Copyright © February 17, 2010 by Gregory J. Matenkoski

All art work, Copyright © February 17, 2010 Gregory J. Matenkoski

Library of Congress Number TXu001672628, all rights reserved, Unless otherwise stated. No part of this book may be reproduced or transmitted in any form or by any means, electronic or mechanical including photo copying, recording or by any information storage and retrieval system without permission in writing from the author.

ISBN 978-0-615-44375-1 ***

LUCKY PENNY'S TAIL

THE TRUE STORY OF EDMUND SURVILLA
Tail Gunner, B-24 Liberator, 453rd BG (H)

By Gregory J. Matenkoski

"Lucky Penny's Tail is a gripping, vivid, first person account. Great and fascinating in detail, the book reads as if one is watching an old war movie."

RICARDO R. VILLARREAL
LAREDO MORNING TIMES

****

"Lucky Penny's Tail, it is real and great."

DOMENIC IMBRIACO
Flight Engineer, top turret, B-24J. 15th A.F., 396th BG (H), Foggia, Italy, February, 1945 to May, 1945.

****

"A rare and welcome insight into a B-24 tailgunner's exploits in the flak-ridden skies above Europe during WWII. This narrative is not about Generals and war strategists, providing instead a well-paced, lively story of one boy's dream to fly, all the while serving his Country in her time of need. This latest addition to the annals of the Greatest Generation is historically relevant, emotionally engaging, intensely gripping in its real-time battle sequences, but above all a tender tribute and heartfelt homage from the author to his dear Friend Edmund Survilla".

HAIG YACOUBIAN
U.S. Navy, USS Constellation, CV-64. Persian Gulf Campaign. Douglas-Boeing Engineering, Operations and Technology, Commercial Support, Boeing, Long Beach, CA.

Dedicated to the heavy bomber crews of the 8th Air Force.

CONTENTS

	Foreword	VII
1	A Simple Life	1
2	Leaving Home	3
3	A Bullet with Wings	8
4	Building a Crew	14
5	The Adventure Begins	21
6	Old Buckenham *(Station #144)*	29
7	Missions	41
	# 1 Siracourt, France	42
	# 2 Gotha, Germany	46
	# 3 Furth, Germany	52
	# 4 Cazaux, France	57
	# 5 Berlin, Germany	59
	# 6 Berlin, Germany	64
	# 7 Brunswick, Germany	73
	# 8 Friedrichshafen, Germany	76
	# 9 Friedrichshafen, Germany	81
	#10 Munster, Germany	84
	#11 Domart, France	87

#12	Pau, France	90
#13	Brunswick, Germany	95
#14	Tutow, *(Rathanow)* Germany	98
#15	Tours, France	102
#16	Tutow, Germany	106
#17	Siracourt, France	108
#18	Watten, France	111
(Make up mission) Siracourt, France		114
#19	Tutow, Germany	118
#20	Siracourt, France	122
#21	Brunswick, Germany	125
#22	Reims, France	130
#23	Orleans, France	133
#24	Troyes, *(Bretzing)* France	135
#25	Merseburg, Germany	139
#26	Lumes, France	143
#27	Romorantin, France	147
#28	Normandy, Invasion Points	152
#29	Normandy, Invasion Points	156
#30	Flers, France	160

	#31	Boulogne, France..165
	#32	Cormeilles, France.............................,.........168
8		That's It Boys, Your Done...............................173

Epilogue..180

Notes..182

A few questions..186

Definitions..188

References...191

Acknowledgements..193

FOREWORD

I was compelled to write this book because of a man I met in 1987. I was twenty-one years old and interested in cars. I wanted to get the tattered seats recovered on my 1970 Dodge.

I went to the local auto upholstery shop where I met a pleasant gray haired man. He was just over six feet tall and wore glasses. I then noticed a model of a Liberator hanging from the ceiling. It was painted in red, white and blue polka dots. I said, "Hey, that's a B-24. Did you fly?"

This man, confident in himself, said with a smile, "Yes." He apparently took an interest in me because I knew what I was looking at.

We started talking and struck a deal. I painted a picture of the plane he flew in World War II on the spare tire cover of his Jeep. *(He wanted it done for his bomb group reunion).* In return, he reupholstered my car seats and, we called it even.

In the twelve years since I met this man, I married, bought a house and moved twice. By chance, I bought another house that was near his place of business.

On Veterans Day 2000, I went to his shop to thank a veteran. It took a moment for him to remember who I was, and then it came back to him. We talked for a while, and then I went about my life.

Because of my interest in military history, I would occasionally stop and visit him at his place of business. I could not pass up the opportunity to hear his stories of aerial combat. It was fascinating to hear accounts I had only read about. Here I was, getting first-hand knowledge of what it was like to fly as part of a WWII bomber crew.

On an April day, I stopped at his shop, and his helper told me he had not been feeling well. Three days later, I went to visit him at his home. From that moment on, I made it a point to see him once a week. It soon turned into three times a week.

For two and a half years, I would visit him faithfully. I'd listen to everything he would say and try to picture all of it in my mind's eye.

I thought it wise to start bringing a tape recorder with me. We eventually taped his life as a WWII airman. He told me everything, good and bad.

This man flew missions before the Allies had achieved Air Superiority over the Third Reich. He was a member of the original cadre that formed the 453rd Bomb Group. He faced the Yellow Nosed, Abbeville Kids. He stubbornly sat through vicious FLAK barrages. His story is common among bomber aircrews, but what an extraordinary duty they performed.

There is nothing romantic about war. For a young man, it is doing a job and the fear of dying. Edmund was one of the many young men that were a part of history. He is a part of a fading light that is nearly out.

I consider myself fortunate to have known this man. I am honored that he considered me, half his age, his friend. This is his story.

Ssgt. Edmund M. Survilla, served in WW II. His Serial number was 33358551. He was the tail gunner of a B-24 Liberator named "Lucky Penny". He was stationed at an airfield named Old Buckenham. Old Buckenham is the name of the hamlet the airfield was located next to. The Air Corps named the airfield, Station #144. Old Buckenham is just outside of the town of Attleboro. Attleboro is located in Norfolk County, East Anglia, England.

Edmund Survilla flew in the 734th Squadron of the 453rd Bomb Group. 2nd Air Division of the 8th Air Force., United States Army Air Corps. European Theater of Operation. Edmund flew combat missions out of Old Buckenham from January, 1944, to June, 1944. Edmund completed thirty-two missions and has one confirmed kill of a Me-109. He and the crew he flew with had a total of seven enemy aircraft destroyed.

The next time you travel by air, look out the window and understand. These bombers flew, and the aircrews fought, five miles above the earth.

LUCKY PENNY'S TAIL

1. A SIMPLE LIFE

My parents named me Edmund and, my family name is Survilla. I was born on March 30, 1923. I have a brother and two sisters. I was raised in the town of Luzerne, PA. Luzerne is in the heart of the anthracite coal region, in the Wyoming Valley of the Appalachian Mountains. Luzerne is near Wilkes-Barre, PA.

I grew up on the top of the hill at 222 Bishop Street. My father was a coal miner who worked long days while my mom tended to us kids. It was a typical depression family.

In my youth, I would always run outside at the sound of an airplane flying overhead. I imagined what it would be like to soar among the clouds. I would build balsa wood and tissue airplanes all the time.

My favorite pastime required sneaking matches from the kitchen to my room. I would grab an airplane, light it on fire then toss it out the window. I would imagine violent WW1 dogfights. I would picture double wingers locked in mortal combat. The German would always take the fatal blow. The model would dive to the ground, crashing in a burning heap.

If I would have been caught doing that, there would have been hell to pay. All I would have heard was, "What are you trying to do? Burn the house down?" We never had a lot of money, but I did have an imagination. I didn't know I was living poor because that was all I knew.

In 1940, the winds of war had stirred a fire in Europe that was consuming the world. I was seventeen years old, 6'2" with hair as black as night. At the time, my world consisted of my brother and I caddying at the nearby Irem Temple Golf Course.

When I would finish for the day, I would wait for my brother. We would then hop on the freight train that came through for a ride home. We would run like two sons-of-bitches to match the speed of it. With a mighty effort, we would pull ourselves aboard.

Sometimes the train would stop at the trestle by the dairy. A tough looking railroad cop would walk the length of the cars looking for problems or hobos. We would hide in a boxcar watching him twirl his Billy club as he came toward us. We would duck in the hope he wouldn't see us. He knew we were there, but he never did throw us off. He knew we were just some local boys hopping a ride home from the golf course.

Sometimes we'd jump off before we would reach the station in Luzerne. That way we could take the shortcut through the neighbor's yard. It usually was a race to the backdoor. It always ended the same, at the kitchen table with dinner on it.

Mom always had dinner waiting for us when we got home. It usually consisted of rice. I ate so much rice I should look like a China Man. There was milk and rice, rice pudding and … oh brother.

I would take 15 cents from the 90 cents I earned each day and give the rest to my mom. The next morning, I would get a ride to the golf course and do it all over again.

I once caddied for a wealthy man that gave me a twenty seven dollar tip. That was a huge amount of money in those days. I gave my caddy master a couple of bucks and told him to buy a beer. I gave my mother the rest. My mom could not believe I made it caddying. She thought I had stolen it. That was a lot of money in those days. That was my life, in the summer of 1940.

2. LEAVING HOME

High school graduation will be soon and I do not want to be here. There are the mines to work for most people, and that is it. I hate the fact that the hard working mentality is taken advantage of by the mine owners.

This is an unsightly mine scarred area. The landscape is dotted with slate banks. It is ugly and it is nothing to be proud of. This may be where I come from, but I do not have to like it.

I will not spend the rest of my days underground. I do not understand how people around here can be proud of making nothing at such a dangerous job. I despise the thought of being like the old timers. I loathe the idea of working underground. I cannot stand the thought of this being my life.

What am I going to do, caddy all my life? There has to be a better way. My family has no money, and I certainly don't have the money to go to college. There isn't any opportunity here. This area is the end of the road. I will leave at the first chance I get.

I will graduate on June 14, 1941. I am then going to leave this place behind. I tell my sweetheart, Helen Menziff, that I have found my opportunity. I have signed up for a civil program. I will learn how to fix airplane engines.

I spend the evening of my graduation on Helen's front porch. I tell her, "Tomorrow morning I will be on my way to Harrisburg, PA". I tell her, "Goodbye."

In the muggy air of the following morning, I hitch a ride to Wilkes-Barre, PA. A train takes me to Harrisburg, PA. There I will begin Engine Basics A&M.

Once I arrive, I am eager to get started. The school building looks like a castle. It is three stories tall, and I stay on the second floor in a room full of bunk beds. All the beds are eventually filled as guys arrive from all over the country. They all share the same story; their town is a dead end. We earn civil service points as we learn a trade.

On December 7th, 1941, Pearl Harbor is attacked. There is no doubt we will be at war. Guys begin to sign up for the service. Everybody feels it is their duty. If you do not, you are considered an outcast. It is more than that though. Most of us guys have no idea what it's like beyond our local towns or cities. This is a chance to get out. This is an opportunity to see exotic places; places you read about. It is a ticket to see the world.

Engine Basics training sends me far from home, to Seymour Johnson Field in South Carolina. I find myself a place to board. The price is right at a funeral directors house so I take it. It isn't too bad of a place; it is quiet and close to the airfield. Tomorrow I will start the next phase in aircraft engine repair.

The training is fun. I like this stuff. I stay at the field after classes all the time to help where I can. I always lend a hand when it comes to changing a rudder, cowl or any little job. I am assigned to take care of supplies. It's not a hands on job, but I am around airplanes.

Congress has declared war and men are being drafted. I manage to get a release from the draft board so I can take the cadet examination. I fail because of my lack of algebra.

The major that heads the airfield asks me, "Why do you want to join the Air Corps?" You could stay here and have a nice life." I tell him, "No sir. All my friends are enlisting; I might as well go too."

The next day, the major tells me, "If you want to fly listen to what I say." He informs me that he has transferred me to New Cumberland, PA. The major hands me three letters. They are from Lieutenant Wanzack, Captain McLear and himself. He instructs me, "You give these letters to only who I tell you to." The next day, I get the orders that put me on a train to New Cumberland.

Upon my arrival the sergeant in charge orders everybody to fall out. I ask him if he would do me a favor. He tells me, "Sure, what's your problem?" I tell him, "No problem sergeant, I have these three letters from the major at Seymour Johnson Field. He instructed me to make sure the executive officer gets them." The sergeant passes the letters on to the proper person. These letters will ensure I get into the Army Air Corps.

The following day, everyone is mustered. There are guys from all over. Hey, two of my friends from back home are here also! The sergeant starts calling names and men begin to fall out. They are being assigned to their part in the war.

My two friends from Luzerne are assigned to tank outfits. *(They survived the war, although one lost an arm and one lost a leg. They were captured by the Germans and wounded when the train they were being transported in was strafed.)*

The sergeant gives me my orders. I am to report to Keesler Field, Biloxi, Mississippi. I will be processed into the USAAC. I am in the Air Corps now and I have the officers at Seymour Johnson to thank. My orders are to leave now. It is November 2nd, 1942.

Keesler Field, Mississippi is a hot, sweaty place. I am one of many airmen learning about aircraft engine repair. We are schooled on inline and radial engines. We are taught about hydraulics and superchargers.

It appears I will be a member of a ground crew. Where will I be stationed, God only knows. It doesn't seem too exciting, but at least I'll be around airplanes. I really wish I had scored better on my cadet exam. After I am certified for engine repair, I am sent to Colorado.

Buckley Airfield, Colorado is where armament school is taught. I know an orderly here. He is from Luzerne also. His name is Glendon Evans. It's nice to know there is somebody from home around here.

As soon as we arrive, all of us guys are put on Kitchen Patrol. All we do is train and go on K.P. It seems I never get a break. I even get stuck with Kitchen Patrol on Christmas Day. This just isn't right.

Just as we finish another shift of K.P., Glendon comes up to the barracks. He barks out, "Is Edmund Survilla here?" Oh no, more K.P. Glendon asks me, "Do you know who I am?" I say, "Yes, sir. You are from my hometown. My father and yours are good friends. Your dad lives a block away from us. He is a mine boss." Glendon tells me to get dressed then report to his office.

When I get there, Glendon does not mess around. He tells me that my father has been killed by a hit and run driver. My heart sinks. All these images flash through my mind. What about my mom? I stand there a moment then blurt out, "What am I supposed to do?" I tell Glendon, "I have just arrived here. I don't have any money; I didn't get a penny's pay yet."

I am told the Red Cross is going to take care of me. They will give me $64.00 to take a train home. I slowly tell Glendon, "It's a long trip, I want to get home quick." He arranges a flight into Pittsburgh, Pa, on a cargo plane. I will then take a train to Luzerne. He will also arrange for a train ride back after my father has been buried.

I am told, "Go, but you have to be back here in a week because classes will be starting." The following day a C-47 transport carries me into the gloomy November sky. My heart is heavy; I do not want to take this sad journey home.

Luzerne is depressing. It is a cold, clammy, wintery day. My mother tells me what happened. Dad was walking along the road in town when a drunk driver ran him over. He just kept going and never did get in trouble. The drunk was a local politician. He left my father to die on the side of a dirty, slushy road. The incident was quietly swept under the rug.

My dad was a World War I veteran. This man fought in the Argonne Forest and won two medals. My father had to be buried but the family does not have any money. Thankfully, the army pays for most of the funeral and the insurance covers the rest.

These are sullen times; I worry for my mother, brother and sisters. I don't want to leave such a bleak situation, but my orders say I have to go. I tell my mother I will send money home. I say my goodbyes, and board the train to Colorado. It is a long, sad ride back to Buckley Field.

As soon as I return, classes begin. We learn our deadly trade. During our training, an instructor announces, "The Air Corps needs gunners for its bombers." He asks if there are any volunteers. He continues, "Anybody that volunteers will be sent to aerial gunnery school at once."

Gunnery school… interesting… a gunner on a bomber. I want to do that. I immediately volunteer along with three friends, Bob Augusta, Tommy Horn and Gil Eagen. Three other guys behind us volunteer also. Only seven out of our class want to fly.

The instructor informs us it will be tough. He asks me if I have good grades. I reply, "Yes, I have good marks but my Algebra background is weak." The instructor tells me I should be O.K. He tells me, "If you study hard and get help when you need it, you should make it."

I have a chance to fly. I have a chance to be an aerial gunner. I have always wanted to fly. This should be exciting. We are told to pack our belongings immediately. Tomorrow, we will be transferred to Laredo, Texas. I want to fly and I am getting my wish.

3. A BULLET WITH WINGS

Laredo, Texas is almost in Mexico. It's hot and dry to say the least. If you're not used to the heat it will beat you up. There are rattlesnakes, scorpions and armadillos all over the place. The rattlesnakes are the worst.

Every time we go out in the morning, they are sunning everywhere. I give them a wide berth when I spot one.

The base has a big two by four and wire mesh cage to keep the rattlers in. Every morning, some crazy guys go around and gather them up. There must be hundreds of them in that cage every day.

The daily training begins with a three-mile run, then calisthenics. After that, it's off to the showers before breakfast. After chow, it's back to the barracks to put on our Class A uniforms. The rest of the morning is spent in the classroom.

After lunch, it's calisthenics for a second time. We run another three miles then go to class again. After dinner, the remaining time is spent on the base until lights out at 9:00 P.M. *(I never did go through boot camp, honest to God. I went to Texas and started class.)*

We have classes seven days a week. Technical sergeants are our instructors. At the end of our daily classes, we are tested on what was taught. At the end of every week, we are tested on what was taught that week.

We are just one week into our training and there are only 35 of 150 volunteers still here. An instructor, a guy in his early forties, tells us, "Pay attention and you will make the grade."

These classes are important. When you get on an aircrew, you had better know your job well. Each crew member has been trained for a specific job and you cannot depend on others to carry you. You may be the difference between the life and death of the whole crew. A failure on your part can ultimately mean the failure of the mission. You had better know your equipment and how it operates. Your life depends on it.

Our training takes us out to the firing range; this is the

stuff I like. The instructors put us in pickup trucks with shotguns. We are told to shoot at clay pigeons as we drive down range. The instructors are evaluating us at our ability to hit moving targets. The first few times we do this it is to see if we can shoot a gun at all.

I get my turn. The truck starts moving. Moments later, a clay bird arcs across the sky. BANG, BANG, the pigeon shatters into pieces and falls to earth. This is fun! Another clay bird goes up, BANG, BANG, it explodes in the sky. The instructor tells us that the fun is over. The next time out we start to keep score. If a guy doesn't score 20 percent hits, he will be washed out.

We work our way up to machine gun training. We are now using the Browning .50 caliber machine gun. It is affectionately known as the Ma Duce. We will use this weapon in combat. It is the standard equipment of the Army Air Corps.

This weapon is a brute. One half inch thick bullets devastate anything they hit. People don't get shot with a .50 caliber round, they get blown apart. The .50 caliber slug penetrates engines, walls, armor; you name it. It is an efficient tool of war.

We go out to the range and learn how to fire these tools of war. The instructor starts us off with stationary targets. We shoot down range then we examine our hits. The instructor tells us why the bullets climb up or run off the target. When we're done, we clean our weapons before they are returned.

We now begin training in what is called flexible gunnery. The firing of any hand held mounted gun is considered flexible gunnery. A waist gunner would fall into this category. The instructor tells us if you are good at dead reckoning, you will be good at this.

The next phase of our training is better yet. The instructors take us flying in AT-6 trainers. The AT-6 is a single-engine aircraft that seats two. The student sits behind the instructor.

We are told; if you have to bail out, stand on your parachute until someone gets you. There are far too many snakes and scorpions to take chances.

The day starts with everybody standing around in their flight gear, holding six-foot long safety straps. There is excitement in the air as each of us wait for our turn to fly.

I am given a barf bag then told, "Let's go." I climb into the back seat and a ground crew member belts me in. The instructor takes us into the sky, and we start to slowly circle the base. He tells me, "Get ready." We start executing slow rolls and diving turns. After we land, I am asked if I feel O.K. I tell my instructor, "I'm good." It was a little rough on the stomach, but I liked it. I can handle this.

We are now given machine guns. When it's my turn, I mount my gun and we takeoff. The instructor takes us to the end of the base, where fly around shooting at ground targets.

The instructors do not keep score. It is to see if we can handle firing a gun in flight. When we finish for the day, the instructors take us fledgling gunners up to the line. We tear down the machine guns, clean and return them.

Now the serious shooting starts. The instructors take us up four at a time in AT-11s. These are twin-engine trainers. They have waist gunner positions that we practice firing from.

We each get a fifty round belt of ammunition. The tips of the bullets are painted a different color for each guy. This is done so we can identify our hits on the target.

The instructors always tell us to drink a bottle of coke and chew some gum so we will not get airsick. Everybody starts walking around chewing big wads of bubblegum.

We begin shooting targets that are towed by another airplane. After we shoot the target up, the tow plane drops it. We run out to them after we land and count our hits. We then report to the instructor. Once again, a minimum of 20 percent hits or you are finished.

It's the same drill over and over. Get your gun; make sure nothing is wrong with it. Get your ammunition, mount the gun and load it. Takeoff, shoot the target, and land. Go out to the target and count your hits. When finished, clean your weapon before you return it. I think I know these guns better than I know my girlfriend. I wonder how Helen is doing. I have to write her.

Today, the instructor tells us we are going to do something new. We are not going to ride in the AT-11s. We are riding in the AT-6 once more. We are issued safety straps once again. Everybody laughs nervously at each other as they chew bubblegum, dragging their safety straps behind them.

The instructor tells me, "Let's go." We walk over to the plane. After mounting the machine gun, I hop in. The instructor hooks up the safety strap then tells me, "Don't puke in the plane." I am asked if I drank my coke as he hands me a barf bag.

The instructor starts the engine and we are off. As we cruise along, I search for the tow target. It appears in the distance below. The instructor asks, "Are you ready?" I answer, "Yes sir." EEEEERRRRRRROOOWWWWWWW, my stomach leaps into my throat as we peel off in a violent, diving turn. Holy crap, the force of the maneuver tosses me half way out of the plane.

Once I get myself orientated, I grab the machine gun. I take aim and shoot the target up as we sweep past it. The next day is the same thing. A person gets used to it quickly. This is exciting, and I get my 20 percent minimum hits on the targets every time.

The class is now introduced to turret training. In the classroom, we learn how each of the turrets operates. The front and tail turrets are nearly identical. We learn the procedures and limitations of turret operation.

We sit in practice turrets to get the feel of them. We spin them around working the guns. If it wasn't so serious, they would make a good ride. I pass all of my tests.

After we receive our manuals and classroom training, we go out to the range again. There is a top turret mounted on the back of a truck. The plexiglas bubble has been removed so the instructor can reach in and work the guns or explain something to us.

I take my turn and climb in. The instructor sits over my shoulder as we ride along. He reminds me, "Watch what your doing. We will be shooting at the tow target. Do not shoot the plane pulling it."

As the truck starts down range, the tow target comes into sight. I pull the trigger, POW, POW, POW, POW. Wow, it's scary at first with those two .50 caliber machine guns going off on either side of your head. It is exciting though.

The instructor tells me this isn't theory anymore. He reminds me how to aim through the optical gun sight. After firing a few more shots, I am reminded again of the concept of the gun sight. I track the target once more. I adjust the control for the lead until the pointers box the target in. POW, POW, POW; hits appear on the tow target.

After the ammo is used up, the tow plane drops the target. The truck carries me to it so I can count my hits. We are told after today all the shooting counts. There will be no cheating. If you do not get a minimum of 20 percent hits in this exercise, you will wash out.

We train daily until we are proficient at the weapons we fire. We are constantly tested ensuring we know our operating systems inside out.

We now have been instructed on the two types of aerial gunnery. Flexible gunnery is given to the guys with good instincts. They will be waist gunners. Turret gunnery is given to the guys that understand the attitude of the aircraft in relation to firing from a turret.

This is training at Laredo, Texas. Of the one hundred fifty guys that volunteered to be aerial gunners, thirty of us make the grade. We have completed the eight weeks of intensive training. We will fly.

Graduation is a proud time. I stand in my Class A uniform as I wait for the ceremony to begin. Boy, my mom would be proud. Some of my fellow graduates have family nearby and they are here to support them.

The band plays as everybody marches onto the parade grounds. We stand at attention as the commanding officer gives us a speech. He then congratulates us on completing our courses. Each of us has our wings pinned on, and then given a handshake.

I have won my wings. An aerial gunner's wings are easy to describe; they are a bullet facing down between spread Eagle wings.

The enlisted men of an aircrew are given the rank of staff or technical sergeant automatically. The Air Corps does this because Herman Goering has a soft spot for airmen. The rank ensures better treatment if captured.

I am an aerial gunner. Bob Augusta, Tommy Horn, Gil Eagen and I are going to fly. Where will we go? What will I fly? Possibly a B-17, maybe a Marauder, but I hear they are a dangerous plane.

The crews call them Flying Whores because there isn't any visible means of support. They say this because the B-26 has a small wing. Hence, no lift. The more fitting name is Widow Maker because of its high stall speed. The Marauder has to be brought in for a landing fast; fast is what the Marauder is all about. Its small wings and big engines make it a hot rod of a bomber.

The next day the entire class is sent to the quartermaster. We are issued our flight gear. Each man receives his jacket, helmet and oxygen mask among other things. Everybody has a graduation picture taken in their flight gear. We are sent from one building to the next, being issued this and signing that.

At the end of the day, we are told to get everything squared away. I just want to go to my bunk. I want to write home to my mom and Helen. I have to tell them that I will fly. I have won my wings. We will be shipping out in two days. I am being sent to Pocatello Field in Idaho.

4. BUILDING A CREW

I am just one of many young airmen assembled at Poocatello Field. We are to be assigned to bomb groups. Some of us will be formed into new aircrews. Some of us will be replacements.

What will I be flying? Will it be the four engine B-17 or B-24. Maybe the twin engine B-25. Will I go to Europe or the Pacific? I can hear guys getting assigned to different bomb groups as their names are called out. They are assigned to groups like the 44th, 98th and the 54th. I don't know what kind of planes these groups fly. I don't know where they are based. It's all Chinese to me.

Edmund Survilla, is shouted out. This tall, skinny guy calls my name. He looks familiar. Holy smoke, this major is the movie star, Jimmy Stewart. (*He talks just like in the movies*). Major Stewart is the operations officer of a newly formed bomb group. "Here," I reply. The major barks out, "Survilla, you are going to be assigned to the 453rd Bomb Group. This is a new bomb group that is flying B-24s. You will be a member of the original cadre. "

I will be a flight engineer in this newly formed group. A fellow airman by the name of George Neamy introduces himself. He tells me he has been assigned to the 453rd also. We pal around until we get our orders. A few days later, we report to Gowan Field in California.

I don't know what's going on at Gowan Field; I just do what they tell me. I will be here for about two weeks. This is where the new crews of the 453rd are being formed. The airmen here do not have to drill or go on K.P. We get our teeth fixed, shots and have other problems addressed. After everybody is taken care of, aircrews will be put together.

It is a nice sunny day as I walk into my assigned barracks. The first guy I introduce myself to is Laddy P. Head. He is a little, dark-haired rebel from North Carolina. He's a gem, a nice guy.

I then meet the other rebel, Robert Hanson. He seems like a politician. He is a big guy, nice guy. Laddy and Rob went to A&M school together.

I shake Joe Craft's hand. He is a big guy, taller than me. He looks like he could be a clown or he could be reserved. He looks like a tough son-of-a-bitch.

I introduce myself to Jim Turwilliger. He is of medium height and build. He tells me he is married and has a child. Jim seems like a quiet guy. He has a family to think about.

Robert Victor and I shake hands. He is on the short side. He is 19 years old, the youngest guy on the crew. The rest of us are in our early 20s.

Hanson says to me, "I guess you will be with me on the flight deck." I reply, "I guess, I was trained to be a flight engineer and they fly in the top turret." He asks me, "Are you married?" I tell him, "No." He tells me he is. I tell Hansen," I am a flight engineer so I should be on the flight deck." I feel sorry for him and tell him to take the top turret.

The odds for survival are less in the tail than on the flight deck but I will take the tail. What's the big deal? If Hansen feels safer on the flight deck, so be it. I'll be a tail gunner.

These are the positions, of the enlisted men, of this potential crew.

> Robert Hanson - top turret.
>
> Laddy Head - ball turret.
>
> Robert Victor - waist gunner.
>
> Jim Turwilliger - waist gunner.
>
> Edumnd Survilla - tail gunner.
>
> Joe Craft is the radio operator.
> *(He does not man a gun.)*

(Our bombardier will be in the nose turret.)

The next day, we meet the officers of our crew. They don't bunk with us; officers stay in their own hut. We meet them in front of our barracks.

Lt. Robert Burgess introduces himself. He is the bombardier. He is a tall, good-looking guy from California. The women must like him.

The pilot is Major Hubbard. He does everything by the book. He is a West Pointer. It is always yes sir, no sir, around him. He will command a squadron. The word is he is a good guy. He never leans on anybody.

The co-pilot is Lieutenant Nick Radosevich. He is a short guy. He was an athlete in college. He is quiet. Maj. Stewart trained Nick. As we get to talking, Nick loosens up.

The navigator is Lieutenant Joe Miller. He is a little guy, quiet. He seems like a nice fellow.

The crew gets to know each other while we are here. Nick is alright, he is one of us. He tells us, "When others are around, you play it by the book." Burgess, Joe Miller and Nick spend their free time together. Victor is always off somewhere; he marches to the beat of his own drum. Hansen and Turwilliger are the married guys of the crew so they pal around. Laddy, Joe Craft and I start running together. Everybody seems to mesh pretty well.

Now that crews have been formed, we are ready to go. The new 453rd members are being sent to March Field in California. We will fly as a crew and see if we are like-minded.

Each new crew is assigned a B-24 to train in. These are bombers that have been through combat. They are too used up for battle, but they work fine for training. The term they use for these planes is war-weary. They all have big white identification numbers painted on them; some still carry their wartime names.

After we arrive at March Field, Maj. Hubbard leaves our crew. He has been assigned to command the 734th squadron. Nick Radosevich is moved to the pilot's seat.

Lieutenant Luther Clark comes to the crew. He is now the co-pilot. He is of medium height and build. He seems like a really nice guy. The crew is now complete.

We train day and night. We practice all hours. We fly touch and goes. We simulate high altitude attacks on any given town. We practice flying preset courses. We constantly drill in formation flying. Our training continuously takes us all over the map.

We feel each other out during these practice missions. We work together well. We are learning to be a heavy bomber crew. Nick and Luther appear to be good pilots. Joe Miller gets us where we need to go and back. Burgess hits the target consistently. We pass the grade. We are officially designated Crew 41.

We are sent to Hamilton Field in California to get our new plane. When we arrive at the Consolidated Plant, Nick accepts delivery of his Liberator. Our plane is a B-24H. The serial number is 42-52169. It is an olive drab upper and light gray lower bomber. We take daily rides as Nick and Luther shake the plane down. They calibrate the instruments and gauges to ensure accurate readings. We stay at Hamilton Field for about a week and a half.

After a week, we are given passes. Hanson, Laddy, Joe Craft and I go to San Francisco. Our main objective is to hit the bars. After a few drinks, we go sightseeing. As we casually walk the streets, we happen upon a pet shop.

A black Cocker Spaniel pup sitting in the window attracts our attention. He looks pretty smart, so we chip in and buy him. We decide to name him Penny. We have our plane and now our mascot.

When we return to March Field, the W.A.C.S. surprise us with a good luck doll. I'll mark all our missions on him. Upon seeing Penny, they make the dog an oxygen mask and jacket. We idle away at March field as our B-24 has its gremlins worked out.

These doldrums have to end. Joe Craft and I concoct a plan. We cut a hole in the fence behind our barracks. We dub it Gate 11. We sneak into town occasionally to get booze or food. We always make sure that the fence looks like it has not been tampered with. Dirt and branches are strewn about to camouflage our unofficial entrance.

The rest of the guys tell us we are going to get caught.

Hah, they are always there for a drink or some food though. None of the other guys have the guts to come along on one of our late night excursions, but nobody would ever rat us out.

Our mission tonight is to sneak into the W.A.C.S. dorm. Joe and I exit the base through Gate 11. Under the cover of darkness, we make our way to the dorm. There isn't anybody downstairs at the desk so we just walk in. We listen for voices as we slowly ascend the stairs. Our goal is the second floor to look for girls. Of course, we find them. We get a thrill watching the girls run around in their panties and nighties.

The girls play coy but some are truly mad. The advisor hears the commotion and comes down the hall. Joe and I hide behind a piano in the corner of the room as the dorm mother searches for us. It's hard to keep from laughing out loud. When she leaves the room, we abort the mission.

We bail out of the second story window. We fall two stories into pricker bushes. Yow, I try to keep it at a whisper as my rear end and the back of my legs are stuck with prickers.

Joe Craft is no better off. We snicker at each other's predicament. We choke down our laughter as we climb out of the bushes. We curse each time we prick ourselves, then laugh at the other's misfortune. No luck tonight, we escape and evade. We make our getaway.

A few days later, we are sent to Morrison Field, Florida. This is where our B-24 is lettered for the bomb group. The American insignias have been painted on at the Consolidated plant. The rest is done here.

We have big white roundels painted on the outer tail surfaces and wing. The letter J is painted inside the roundels in black. The letter J designates the 453rd Bomb Group. On the tail surface, under the roundels, the serial number is painted in white. Under the serial number is a J+ painted in white. This is the plane's radio call letter. E8 is painted aft of the waist gunner's window. This is the designation of the 734th Squadron.

Nick decides to name our B-24 after the dog. "Lucky

Penny" is the name of our bomber. The ground crew gets on it right away. A black Cocker Spaniel riding a bomb is painted on the left side of the plane between the cockpit and the nose. The name, "Lucky Penny" is written above the dog in white. We each write our names under the top turret in white.

We are ordered to Tindal Field, Florida, for jungle training. It is assumed we are going to the Pacific. We fly daily navigational missions with the other bombers up and down the coast.

There is nothing to do on the ground except worry about snakes and gators. We live in ragged tents and develop rashes from bug infestations. The itching drives us nuts. We fly out of Tindal for about a week.

We are ordered back to Morrison Field for a few days. We are deloused and our clothes are burned in a huge bonfire. After we are issued new gear, our orders take us to Midland, Texas.

As soon as we touch down in Midland, we are caught in a snowstorm. We are snowbound. We are grounded for eight days. We cannot go anywhere. We just sit around in our barracks. It is absolutely boring, we cannot leave soon enough. We will make our way to the East Coast when everything clears up.

Why we go where we go, I don't know. After we escape Texas, we stop over in Tennessee. Joe Craft and I go to Memphis on our leave. We go to a bar and tie one on. In our drunken wisdom, we decide to rent roller skates. We skate the sidewalks of Memphis at midnight. Realizing it is late and we have to get back, we leave the skates in the gutter. We take a taxi back to the base in time.

In the morning light, we fly back to Morrison Field. After we touch down, we are told we will receive our orders for combat. There is apprehension in the air.

The rest of the day is spent loading Penny for her journey overseas. The bomb bay is packed with clothes, duffle bags, boxes, parachutes you name it.

The plane will be carrying fourteen people. It is only right that Major Hubbard flies with us. He was our original pilot. His assistant, the flight Sergeant and our crew chief, Sergeant Twibell, will fly with us also. Last but not least, our dog, Penny.

We are given sealed orders and a compass heading. We will fly with two other B-24s. We will fly in a three-plane formation so an aircraft is not alone if a problem should arise. We roll down the runway into the early morning darkness, goodbye America.

We are on our way. This is just the beginning of a new adventure for this young man. I momentarily entertain the thought of not coming back. Did I make the right decision in my life? After we are in the air for an hour, Nick opens our orders.

The orders in short read:

> E.T.O., *(European Theater of Operation)*, Depart from Florida to Natal, Brazil. Cross the Atlantic to North Africa. From North Africa continue to Valley, Wales. From Wales proceed to your base in England.

We will be fighting Hitler. We are taking the southern route to England. I'm sure Major Hubbard knew where we are going all along.

5. THE ADVENTURE BEGINS

We fly into the waning darkness, uncertain of our future. The only visible signs of our three-plane formation are the glowing exhaust tips of the engines. The night conceals the direction we are going. What will happen in Europe? Silhouettes of the other two Liberators emerge as dawn breaks on the horizon. We journey to Natal.

The comforting drone of the engines is disrupted by the sound of one of them breaking up. The gauges tell the story. Nick informs us we have an oil pressure issue. We will have to put Penny down.

Lt. Miller plots a course to the nearest base. We will divert to Waller Field, Trinidad. Our three-plane formation sets course for the emergency strip. We land on one of the two simple runways carved out of the jungle.

The aircrews of the accompanying Liberators linger around the barracks. They have nothing to do except to wait for us. They try to settle into the roofless primitive huts. How is anyone supposed to be safe from the elements in these shacks? No matter, we get to work.

This is only an emergency strip. Thank God, Sergeant Twibell is with us. There is no support here. We will have to tear the engine down ourselves. The culprit is a collapsed oil pump. We will have to wait for a new one to be delivered. We will install it ourselves. All we can do is wait for the pump to arrive.

Nights are spent on the floors of these concrete huts. The enlisted men take turns pulling guard duty; this is standard procedure. Everybody likes the Tommy Gun. Laddy and I argue over it every time. The loser ends up with the carbine.

The enemies we guard against are boa constrictors and all kinds of bugs. After dark, the hyenas come out. Their laughter can be heard all night. I will put a bullet in one of them the first chance I get.

On the fifth day, a C-47 delivers our oil pump. We can finally put Penny back together. By evening, she is ready to go. Just before sundown, the three bombers of our little formation sit idling at the end of the runway. The engines are run up, and everything checks out good. We are ready to continue to Natal.

The pilot of the lead plane gets the rpm's up and lets the brakes go. The four engines scream as the bomber thunders down the strip. Oh no, he does not have enough speed to takeoff. The pilot pulls on the yoke in a desperate attempt to get airborne. Just before the B-24 reaches the end of the runway, the front wheel lifts off the ground. The plane struggles for a moment then plows into the earth. The doomed bomber leaves a huge furrow in its path.

A person can see things that the mind really cannot comprehend. The Liberator crashes at the end of the runway and erupts into flames. From the nose to the cockpit, the plane is a twisted, mangled wreck. From the cockpit back, the plane is engulfed in a high-octane fire. The pilot and co-pilot thrash wildly as their belts keep them strapped in their flaming coffin. The bodies finally contort in horrific convulsions of death. Nobody lives through that.

Suddenly, the navigator claws his way out of a gash torn in the mangled nose. Fighting for his life, he staggers away from the burning hulk. He stumbles, stops and sits on the outer wing of the blazing bomber. He sits there as the flames slowly creep up to and catch him. He does not attempt to escape as he is engulfed in fire.

Incredible, he just sits there motionless and burns with the plane. The poor bastard must have been knocked silly. Penny is silent at the sight of this macabre spectacle. Consumed by the flames, the navigator finally tips over. There he burns.

Major Hubbard tells Nick, "Let's go. Don't worry about that plane. Let's get moving before it explodes." Nick guns the throttles. Moments later, Penny leaps over the burning hulk that lights the end of the runway.

Major Hubbard instructs Joe Craft to radio the proper authorities. There will be people along to take care of the remains. Will the next of kin be told the true nature of their loved one's death, or will they be told the men were killed in action? It's better off they are told they were killed in the line of duty. Let the families have some solace.

Our two ship formation flies to Natal, Brazil. What we just witnessed lays heavy on our minds. In mid flight, we are diverted to the naval base in Belem, Brazil. We land in Belem on Christmas Day 1943. We are ordered to stand down. We will be here for a little over a week.

Belem is a primitive place. It is hot and it stinks like a garbage dump. We live in tents on wooden floors. We have the daily option of going to the village or the beach. Most of our time is spent swimming at the beach.

Every day, Laddy, Joe and I go to the village on booze runs. It is unbelievable the things that go on there. Brothers prostitute their little sisters. Kids sell monkeys, snakes, birds, you name it. They will do anything to make a buck in this dump of a place. We purchase our liquor and return to the beach.

On our next visit into the village, we decide to buy a monkey. They are small; they could fit inside your shirt. We figure what the hell, we'll buy two. These monkeys will make good mascots. We pay the kid and leave.

The day before we continue our Atlantic crossing, Joe Craft finds a cooler. We cut up all kinds of fruit and throw it in. We gather the leftover booze and make one potent punch. The cooler is then strategically placed in the rear of the plane. The rest of the evening is spent preparing "Lucky Penny" for the flight overseas.

A voice brings me from my slumber, "Wake up, it's time to go." We get ready for takeoff. All the cargo is balanced and everything is buttoned up. Everybody piles in the plane. Sergeant Twibell stands watch as Nick and Luther fire up the engines. They are run up then set back to idle. Everything looks good.

Our two-plane formation taxis to the end of the ramp. Nick turns Penny on the runway and guns the throttles. We lumber down the strip as Penny gathers speed. With a nudge on the yoke, we leap into the sky. Moments later, the second B-24 joins us. The naval base fades into the hazy distance.

We are on our way, fourteen men, a dog, a bomb bay

full of cargo and two monkeys. Our two-ship formation begins its Atlantic crossing. Laddy. Joe Craft and I retire to the cooler as soon as we reach our cruising altitude.

We pass the time slowly getting drunk. Sergeant Twibell figures out what we are doing, and asks for a drink. In our drunken generosity, he is accommodated. Our crew chief disappears forward with a cup full of punch. He returns repeatedly for more of the spiked concoction he speaks so highly of. As time passes, the drone of the bomber's engines finally lures us to sleep.

I awake with a pounding headache. Laddy does not look any better than I feel. He looks green around the edges. Joe Craft looks like he is ready to puke. I feel like shit. Laddy grabs his mask and begins to gulp down oxygen. Not a bad idea, we follow his example. Our heads are cleared of mind numbing hangovers after sucking down some oxygen.

Flying over the ocean is mesmerizing. On a cloudless day, the sea and sky merge into one, endless. There aren't any landmarks. There is only the occasional ship at sea. They look so lonely in the vast expanse below. We are totally dependant on Miller's navigation skills.

Five hours into the flight, we develop a problem of a different sort. The monkeys start running amok through the plane. One of them will not leave Luther alone. It constantly irritates him, jumping around his shoulders and climbing over his face.

Luther shoos it away, but the monkey refuses to leave. The angrier Luther gets, the more Nick laughs at him. Finally, Luther yells out, "Get this god damn monkey out of here!" The monkey jumps out of the way, as Luther takes another swipe at it. It scurries to the back of the plane. We catch him and "BOMBS AWAY," out the bomb bay it goes. The other monkey immediately settles down.

Victor, Turwilliger, Laddy and I spend our time in the waist gunner's positions. I occasionally go back to my turret and look around. The accompanying B-24 flies on our wing. Will they make it? Will we make it?

Thoughts of home fill my mind. I think about Helen. I

wonder what I'm getting into. People are dying, but that will not happen to me. Nick announces we are minutes from Dakar, North Africa. We have just enough fuel to make it. Miller is good. He has guided us right in.

Dakar is an eye opener. It is hot and dusty. It is a dirty, crummy place with primitive outhouses. The horse flies are so big they could carry you away. After Penny is shut down, we secure her. We are directed to the mess hall for something to eat.

The cook is a Frenchman, and the natives that run the mess hall are in the French Army. They look dirty and sickly. They are skinny, and their robes hang on them like rags. The whole place reeks.

We sit and look around in disgust at the condition of this place. Not one of us will eat the food we are served. I think it is supposed to be Chicken-a-la-King. It's more like Chicken-a-la-Crap. We just stare at the mess we are served. It is made with some kind of meat. The food is covered with maggots and little black things.

Burgess grumbles," What the hell is this?" He walks into the kitchen to confront the cook. We wait to see the outcome as the cook takes him out the side door. Burgess comes back waving his hands in a no gesture. "Don't eat it," he warns us shaking his head. He tells us, "Take a look outside." Our bombardier leads us around the side of the building. He points to a pile of feathers. What the..., seagulls? We immediately grab our trays and dump the maggot-infested crap out.

The natives appear out of nowhere. They start picking the garbage out of the trashcans. Coffee grinds, food, whatever. They are poor; food is food.

We settle for black bread and jam. We will have to put up with this for a day and a half. We'll be here just long enough to get sick in this disease infested place. We decide to stay with the plane until it's time to leave.

We finally get the orders out of here. The fuel truck has gassed us up, and the engines have been turned. Before we takeoff, Sgt. Twibell checks Penny over one last time. Major Hubbard shouts out, "Let's go." After everybody gets their flight gear on, we climb aboard. The engines are run up and the two bombers taxi out. Our destination is Marrakech. We can't get out of here soon enough. Good riddance to this shit hole called Dakar.

We make Marrakech in a few hours. It is a hot, dusty place. The wind smacks our faces as we emerge from under the B-24. I am told it gets up to 101 degrees in the day then falls to below freezing at night. We secure Penny before Sgt. Twibell brings the dust covers out of the hold.

Penny must be covered before the wind driven sand damages her. The engines, vents, pitot tube and glass are covered immediately. The bomb bay stays closed in this hostile environment. If our Liberator wasn't buttoned up, there would be sand in everything. So..., this is Marrakech, North Africa.

We are informed we are in a war zone now but we do not see anything in the way of the enemy. Rommel's vaunted Africa Corps was smashed in May. Patton and Montgomery have already marched from here to Italy. The Italians were liberated a few months ago. The 15th Air Force has already started operations out of there.

Tattered and sun bleached tents are what we live in. The mess hall here is an old hanger with no roof. What is it with no roofs? The food is terrible, no better than the stuff at Dakar.

There are a lot of Muslims here. They wear white robes and ride camels. They do a lot of singing and dancing. They are looking to trade with anybody that looks their way.

We, on the other hand, spend our time practicing takeoffs and landings. Our guns have to be constantly cleaned because of the sand. We will have to put up with this nonsense for about ten days.

It seems like Laddy and I are always pulling guard duty. We have to do this. We are told, "Be aware, the Muslims pretend to be our friends." They try to act affable in an attempt to get close to the planes. They come around day and night; they try to distract us with dancing or conversation.

They are the enemy. They have a nasty habit of jamming grenades inside the engine nacelles. They like pulling the pins and holding the spoons on them. They then wedge the grenade between the engine and the housing. They do this hoping the grenade vibrates loose while the plane is in flight, blowing it out of the sky. They do respect the business end of a Tommy gun though.

The guys do not like sleeping in the tents. They do not feel safe. They wait to have their throats cut. The crew starts to sleep in the plane. The other crew does the same. Everybody feels safe inside their guarded B-24.

Our orders have arrived. We can leave Marrakech. All of the gunners are issued 25 rounds of ammunition. The weapons are checked once more, ensuring everything is in proper working order. I split my belt in two before I put the rounds in the ammunition feed track. Once we are airborne, I'll charge my guns. The engines have been turned, and Penny is ready.

Nick and Luther go through the checklist and bring Penny to life. The two bombers taxi to the end of the strip. Our pilot turns Penny onto the runway. After making sure the nose gear is straight, he guns the throttles. Penny crabs into the crosswind and we are off.

Our orders take us to Valley, Wales. Once we reach cruising altitude, I man my turret. Nick tells us to check our guns. I push the tit on my control stick, POW, POW, POW. Wow, the first time I fired these guns in a war zone. Everybody lets a few rounds loose. We are ready for action. Maybe I'll get me a German.

I strap on my throat mic and clean my sunglasses. A quick search reveals an empty sky. Our two-ship formation flies to its next destination. A look into the deteriorating western sky obscures the sun. It appears the weather will not cooperate with us. The closer we get to Valley, Wales, the worse it is. Miller puts us on a course for the small airfield there.

Valley, Wales, is a damp, cool place, at least in the winter months. It is on the southwest corner of Great Britain. Valley takes all the abuse the Atlantic gives it. The ocean currents always make it damp and foggy.

"Lucky Penny" has a hell of a time finding the airstrip in the fog. There isn't a beacon at the end of the runway, but Nick and Luther put us down safe. Once again, Joe Miller gets us where we need to go. He is pretty good.

We are directed to a hardstand where Nick shuts our Liberator down. After emerging from the bomb bay, Crew 41 stretches out. Before we get our flight gear off, we are handed two hour passes. We hop into the back of a Duce and a Half that takes us to a little pub down the road.

The bar is a dingy little place. You are allowed talk with the locals but if they ask you any questions, you cannot answer them. They are nice people though. After a few drinks, it is back to the truck.

We ride back to our plane in the darkness. The truck suddenly stops with a jolt. The driver starts yelling, "Everybody out, everybody out!" What is going on? German bombers have apparently been spotted coming this way. My knees are tingling, and a shiver runs down my spine. I want off now. We hastily jump from the truck into a ditch alongside the road.

This is crazy. Will I have a bomb dropped on me before I even fly a mission? It is scary, but luck is with us, nothing happens. Planes can be heard in the distance, that is all. We get back on the truck and return to the airfield. We are told we will be staying here for a few days.

With my free time, I write home to Helen and mom. It has been a while. I'm sure they would like to know how I am doing. I'll mail the letters when we get to our base in England.

After a few days of doing nothing, we prepare Penny for the final leg of her journey. It is time to get to our base. The people are nice, but there is no war to be fought here.

Penny carries us down the runway into a gray, somber sky. We are off to our new home. We are flying to a place called Old Buckenham. It is near a town called Attleboro in England.

6. OLD BUCKENHAM *(Station #144)*

The airbase, Old Buckenham, is carved out of lush farmland. Its military designation is Station #144. The base gets its moniker from a nearby hamlet named Old Buckenham. This hamlet is a crossroads and houses. It sits about two miles from the base. Old Buckenham is near the town of Attleboro. This town's biggest asset is the train station. Attleboro is located in Norfolk County, East Anglia. Attleboro is about 80 miles northeast of London, England.

We approach the airbase from the south. It is a work in progress. The main runway is laid out in a southwest to northeast direction. It is 6,000 feet long. The main beacon for the base is at the southern end of this strip. There is a windmill that stands out there too.

There are two auxiliary runways. They are both 4,200 feet long. One points north and the other northwest from my point of view. The way the three strips are laid out form a triangle. The auxiliary runways are to the left of the main strip.

The taxi ramp outlines all three runways. There are two hangers for the bombers along the ramps. They face to the south and west of the runways. The hardstands ring the strips. The bomb dump is situated at the northern end of the airfield. The aviation fuel tanks sit to the east.

The living quarters are to the west of the runways. The base offices and hospital are closest. This is where operations are run from. The briefing buildings are in this area also. The parachute hanger is nearby. All the buildings that are vital to the operation of the base are closest to the runways.

Next are the communal areas. Each of the four squadrons has their own. There are the officer and enlisted men clubs. There is space for athletic activity just about anywhere.

The living quarters are located furthest from the runways. They are corrugated Nissen huts. Each squadron is situated in its own area. Each squadron has their own mess halls and latrines.

We touch down at our newly operational airfield. We are directed to our hardstand. Our ground crew is here to meet us. They arrived a two weeks earlier by ship. They have already set up shop in anticipation of our arrival.

We step out onto the muddy, frozen, incomplete base. The critical components for flight operations are finished though. The runways, taxi ramps and hardstands are fresh concrete. There are a few finished roads, but the rest is mud. This is where the men of the 453rd are going to live. From here we will go off to fight, and some of us will die.

Liberators arrive daily. About a third of each squadron is here. They come in groups of three. "Lucky Penny" takes her assigned place in the 734th Squadron.

A jeep pulls up to take Major Hubbard, his assistant and the flight surgeon to their offices. Major Hubbard has to prepare the squadron. Sgt. Twibell joins his men.

We load our gear on the truck that waits for us. We are driven to the barracks area. Here is where the enlisted men of Crew 41 will live. All of the enlisted aircrews sleep together. The officers stay in their own barracks, but they have the same arrangements. We have our pick of any empty Nissen hut. We choose the corrugated shack at the end of the road to be our home.

As we stow our gear away, an orderly opens the door, and another crew looks inside. Hey, it's George Neamy! I know him from training. We shake hands then shoot the breeze for a moment. He tells me he is a member of the Carter crew. They will stay in the same hut with us. That's good, George is a good guy. The crews introduce themselves then pick beds.

The huts have a front and back door. There is a separate room in the back. It is nice, but it comes with a price. The guy that takes this room is in charge of the barracks. George Neamy takes it. Our crew takes the front of the hut. We all have lockers along with a place to stow our clothing and flight gear. My bunk is under a window.

In the middle of the hut is a pot bellied stove. This is our source of heat. We will need to gather our own timber to supplement our ration of coal. We make a pile of wood next to the hut. God help anybody if they lay a finger on it.

After we settle into our barracks, we are shown the rest of the base. We are directed to the mess halls. Each squadron has two. There is one for the aircrews and the other is for the ground crews. The aircrew mess is open 24-hours a day.

The mode of transportation around the base is by bicycle. When guys ride up to their barracks, they like to jump off of their bikes and let them go. The bike makes a knock, knock, knock, knock, knock, knock sound as the handlebars slide over the corrugated metal of their hut. We are told it can be irritating when you are trying to sleep. It can down right startle you sometimes.

As we tour our new home, a few bombers takeoff into the cold January sky. These crews have arrived earlier. They are flying practice missions. The 453rd has yet to become operational.

I finally understand the reason for all of the layovers on our way here. This was a stall tactic to let the engineers complete more of the airfield. More time was needed to construct hardstands and such.

There are still many semi-frozen mud paths that criss-cross the base. Pallets and boards act as bridges spanning the mires. After a day of orientation, a tired crew hits the sack.

We go out to the plane daily, as does the ground crew. We constantly go over it. We spend the majority of our time cleaning the guns. We constantly fly practice missions all over England. We always fly fully armed. We have to; we are in a war zone, anything could happen. It is boring, but we are preparing for combat.

The ground crew installs gun cameras in Penny's turrets. A few of the bombers in the group have been equipped with them. The brass wants to see what is going on over enemy territory. Fighters can't go all the way with us on the deep missions, so we carry the gun cameras.

After our daily dry runs, we sit around the barracks with a monkey, and sometimes the dog. The dog splits time between the officer's hut and ours. I am beginning to really hate these practice missions. We are not here to fly around the countryside of East Anglia. We are here to fight.

Alerted; February 4, Search and rescue mission. We are finally going to see some action. At the briefing, we are told that one of the 453rd's B-24s has gone down in the North Sea. "Lucky Penny" will be part of a small formation that will go search for this lost plane. The crew is edgy but excited. This will be our first flight in action. There is always a chance of seeing enemy fighters.

Under a cold, gray sky, we walk over to the parachute hanger. This better work, I think to myself, as I grab my chute. We stand around with the other aircrews waiting for the trucks to take us to the bombers. A big old Duce and a Half rolls up and takes us out to Penny.

This is exciting, we pitch our flight gear off the truck as we pull up to the plane. We suit up while Nick briefs us with final instructions. Nick and Luther climb aboard Penny to start the preflight checklist.

The process starts. Controls are unlocked then the gyros are uncaged. Everybody gets in Penny except me. I wait under the wing while Nick starts the engines. I am a flight engineer and I like doing this. I watch for fires or obvious problems during start up. Luther yells out, "Clear on three." The engine coughs to life. Each engine coughs to life before it winds up to a solid roar.

Satisfied, I climb up through the bomb bay to the flight deck. Nick sets the engines at a steady idle before he runs them up. All the gauges check out. The bomb bay doors are closed and the wheel chocks are pulled. We taxi out down the flight line. We join the search formation idling at the end of the runway. We sit, waiting to takeoff.

A flare arcing across the sky is our signal to go. The lead ship is off. Every 30 seconds, another B-24 rolls down the runway. When it's our turn, Nick revs up the engines for a final reading. The gauges look good. The flaps are set and the brakes are released.

Nick swings onto the runway without stopping. Our

pilot guns Penny's throttles as we start to roll. He gently works the rudder pedals keeping the bomber straight. Luther watches the gauges while he reads off the miles per hour. Hansen watches the gauges also. He pays attention to the hydraulics and fuel transfer lines, among other things. Penny thunders down the runway. Luther calls out, "One hundred thirty miles per hour." Nick eases the yoke back a hair. "Lucky Penny" leaves the ground behind as she climbs into the dreary, gray overcast.

Four propellers pull us skyward. Luther watches the manifold pressure as he retracts the landing gear. He slowly raises the flaps as we gain air speed. Once Penny is clean, we start a circling climb until we join the waiting aircraft.

Nick takes Penny a little higher than the formation. He puts her in a shallow dive and slides our B-24 into her assigned place among the bombers. We continue to circle until the remainder of the search party forms up.

Joe Craft gives me the thumbs up as I go to man my station. I hop on the catwalk that takes me through an empty bomb bay. Laddy Head climbs into his turret as I step around the well. Turwillger and Victor help him before they man their waist guns. I step over the escape hatch to the tail of the plane. I sit down on my little seat and unlock the turret. I work the guns as I search the skies.

After the remaining bombers form up, we fly in a loose formation into the overcast. The lead navigator sets our course. Miller sets his own, just in case. Burgess climbs in the nose turret; his eyes are peeled as he searches for enemy fighters.

The formation reaches the last radioed position of the downed B-24. The planes fan out and start flying a search pattern. The weather is terrible; visibility is poor at best.

Nick takes Penny down to 50 feet. We are really on the deck. White caps leap up at us from an angry sea. The prop wash shoots a spray all over the back of the plane. It gives the effect of a driving rain hitting my turret.

We fly over sunken ships that are plainly visible from above. We pass over the occasional sea mine bobbing on the surface of a raging sea. Tether broken, they drift aimlessly about. The formation searches a good five hours. There is nothing, nothing at all. The sea is too rough and cold to survive. This crew is lost. We climb to altitude before we head back.

Once we return to Old Buck, we get into a holding pattern and wait our turn to set Penny down. Ten minutes later, we are on the ground. Nick opens the bomb bay as we taxi to our hardstand. After the propellers come to a stop, we emerge from under our Liberator.

Major Stewart drives out to get a report from Nick. The officers pile in the major's jeep, and drive away. The truck pulls up for us moments later. We are debriefed before we head to the mess hall for something to eat.

It has been a long, frustrating day. We return to our hut tired out. I write an entry in my diary. I will keep this diary to chronicle my life. If I should die, my family will at least know something of what I did. If I make it, I will have this for memories when I grow old. I say my prayers before I hit the rack.

Alerted, February 6th, Siracourt, France, We will attack coastal batteries. This is our first real mission. In briefing, we are told we are going to take it to the enemy. Oh boy, what will it be like?

We grab our gear then head to the plane. The ground crew has laced two extra boxes of ammo into the feed track as requested. I ask if they cut an onion in half and rubbed it on the turret glass. A vet told me to do this; it keeps the glass from frosting over.

The engines sound strong as Nick and Luther bring Penny to life. Our bomber is ready to go. We join the procession that taxis to the end of the runway. A flare arcing across the sky is the groups signal to go.

The first Liberator revs up and thunders into the sky. Before the first one is airborne, the next B-24 starts rolling. This is pretty impressive. Five more planes, then we will be on our way.

The next Liberator to roll down the strip has a problem.

Oh no, this plane does not have enough speed and it crashes at the end of the runway. No fire, just a crumpled wreck. Agonizing seconds later, the full bomb load explodes like nothing I have ever seen. No fireball, just a huge explosion. Nothing can live through that.

The 453rd keeps a big bulldozer at the end of the runway for such accidents. This dozer has a thirty-foot blade on it. The guy that drives this beast clears the runway of wrecks. Pieces of what once was a Liberator shower from the sky. Before all the pieces hit the ground, emergency crews go into action. The dozer then pushes what is left of this plane and crew out of the way.

Takeoffs are diverted to the auxiliary runway. There is a mission to fly. There are twelve more planes waiting to takeoff. There is a formation waiting in the sky using fuel. There are fighters to rendezvous with. The dozer makes a few passes before the main strip is operational again.

Nick brings Penny on to the auxiliary runway. Without stopping, he guns the throttles. Penny makes all kinds of noise as she hurls down the strip. The engines vibrate through the plane as they scream at full power. On Nick's command, they pull us into the sky.

The snow-blanketed countryside comes into view as we climb to join the group. The dark colored runway stands in stark contrast against a white background. It vanishes as we climb into the overcast.

Visibility is poor in this dreary sky. The weather makes forming the group together difficult. It is sloppy at best. Some planes nearly collide. We suffer through tense moments until we break out above the clouds. The formation heads out over the channel for Siracourt.

The view from my turret is crystal clear. The onion trick works, who would have thought. I always wear sunglasses and leave my goggles on top of my head. It's just something that works for me. Even though there are tinted panels of plexiglas, I like the extra protection from the sun.

After I get situated in the turret, I work the guns. Nick tells the crew to get on oxygen. I strap on my mask then plug into the feed. Next, the throat mic is plugged into the intercom. Everybody checks in to confirm they are on oxygen and everything is working properly.

Penny climbs to a cruising altitude of 28,000 feet. The sky is a bright azure blue. The only thing visible below is a blanket of white, puffy clouds. The cloud cover stretches as far as I can see. The bombers are insignificant in the midst of such a vast expanse.

It is cold up here, 30 to 60 below zero. Those fleece-lined boots stink so I wear my dress shoes. For how those boots look you would think they would be warmer than my shoes. Extra socks do the trick. It's dress shoes for me until they issue better boots.

It's the same deal with the bomber jackets; they are fleece lined pieces of crap. They look nice and all, but they are no good up here. The crew wears mechanic's jumpsuits. We layer our clothes underneath them. The layering is superior for warmth. They are more comfortable and give you more freedom of movement; most crews prefer the jumpsuits

Turwilliger and Victor wear parkas at their waist positions. Their hoods are up in their battle against the biting cold. They also wear the heavy felt lined pants. They need to wear goggles against the elements. Their stations are opened to the rarified atmosphere.

Everybody wears gloves. If you touch anything bare handed you will rip your skin off. Everything on your body is covered, but the cold still saps the energy from you. Frostbite can find its way into fingers or toes.

You have to be careful with your oxygen mask at altitude. Condensation can build up on the edges of it. Your mask can freeze to your face. You can tear the skin off when you adjust it and not even know it happened.

The recall comes over the intercom. The mission has been scrubbed due to weather. Primary and secondary targets are socked in. It is a solid blanket of white below. The bombers set course for home.

The 453rd returns with full bomb loads. All the planes come down through the gray overcast without incident. Nick brings our bomber to the hardstand. We emerge from

Penny irritated. All of this tension for nothing. Worst of all, this mission does not count. There will be no bomb painted on Penny today. We go debrief before we look for a way to get the chill out of our bones.

Alerted; February 10th, Gilze-Rigen, Holland: Airfield. Here we go again. Maybe we'll see some action this time. We wait while Nick does the preflight checklist. Hansen sticks his head out of the flight deck escape hatch to watch our co-pilot work the control surfaces.

After Luther exercises the ailerons, elevators and rudders, Nick goes down the list to engine start up. I wait in Penny's shadow as each engine is turned over. I do like the rush of wind on my face as they start.

After I climb aboard the crew chief directs us off the hardstand. We fall into the line of bombers that taxi to the end of the ramp. With a roar of the engines, we start our run. Nick works the throttles to keep Penny straight as we thunder down the strip. Crabbing as we takeoff, he turns the nose of the plane into the crosswind, Penny forces her way into the sky.

The surrounding bases come into view as we climb into position. I watch one of our neighboring bomb groups launch its B-17s for the raid.

Oh no, here we go again. A Flying Fortress crashes, skidding to the end of the runway. Men start to run for their lives as the wreck begins to spew black, acrid, smoke. In a brilliant flash, the B-17's full bomb load violently explodes. A visible shock wave rocks the end of the runway. Better them than me.

The 453rd forms up behind its rally ship. This is a yellow and olive drab checkerboard painted B-24. "Wham Bam" is the name of this gaudy airplane. It is supposed to look like this for easy identification; it is a flying circus wagon, to say the least.

A rally ship is used to prevent mistakes in formation assembly. Each group has their own unique plane. The paint jobs range from stripes to polka dots. A group follows their rally ship to their assigned place in a formation. Once they are positioned, the rally ship peels off. It will now fly circuits over the North Sea acting as a radio relay for that particular bomb group. After the raid, each group will follow their rally ship back to their base.

Fighters emerge from the distance, they settle in along side of us. Spitfires, they are a pretty plane. They will escort us as far as they are able. At the coast of France, Nick reports FLAK ahead. Oh boy, here we go! I have been told about the hazards of this FLAK.

The German 88mm artillery piece is a versatile, high velocity weapon. This cannon fires the anti-aircraft shells that darkens the sky. The 88mm cannon, I am told, has no problem firing shells beyond our altitude.

The enemy shoots at us but I cannot see the barrage from the tail. It is out ahead of the formation. Nick announces, "Target obscured, mission scrubbed."

I get a look at this FLAK as we turn for home. A black curtain hangs in the sky. We were supposed to fly through that? Jesus Christ, what the hell am I getting into? Apprehension washes over me as we return to England.

The 453rd follows "Wham Bam" back to Old Buck. The planes take up a racetrack pattern over the base as they wait to land. After each lap, a plane comes in. After circling for ten minutes, Nick sets Penny down.

Two times out, and this mission doesn't count either. After debriefing, we get something to eat before we make our way to the hut. The stove needs loaded; it will be cold in there. The fire is nearly out every time we come back.

We walk into a full-blown mess. What the hell happened in here? All of our belongings are knocked off the shelves. There are clothes scattered everywhere. All the care packages are opened and strewn about.

The culprit sits on a shelf looking at us. The monkey has wrecked the place. George Namey snaps, "Get that god damn monkey out of here." Everybody is angered over the mess. The monkey is grabbed and tossed out the door. Once we clean up, we finally get to sleep.

When we are awakened for the mission, one of the guys calls us outside. "You have to see this," he exclaims.

Everybody steps into the darkness. There the monkey sits next to the door, frozen stiff. It is clinically examined then tossed into the garbage. We will not have to worry about destroyed care packages anymore

Alerted; February 11th, Hambures, France: Target, construction of installations. Here we go again. Maybe we will get credit for a mission for once. We are briefed then trucked out to Penny. The crew is itching for some action. We put on our gear under Penny's wing. After the preflight rituals, everybody climbs aboard for engine startup.

It can be spooky at times entering the plane through the bomb bay. The bombs hang ominously from the racks. They have their safety pins in but it is still eerie. The fuel transfer lines are inspected as I climb to the flight deck. Everything checks out O.K. Nick takes Penny off her pad.

We join the procession taxiing down the ramp. Nick keeps the momentum going forward when we turn onto the runway. He jams the throttles forward as we start our run down the strip. Riding a tail wind, Penny leaps into the sky. We climb to our place in the formation that will bring destruction to Hambures.

The view is stunning as fighters fly above us. The planes around me pull contrails. This happens when the hot, humid air from the engines exhaust condenses in the cold air. The formation leaves white, ice crystal trails across the heavens. How could the Germans miss us?

I glimpse the other bombers as we fly in combat formation. Four engine machines of war wing across the sky. Turrets turn and guns move around searching for the enemy. Pilots take care not to collide with surrounding bombers. The Spitfires peel off having gone to their limit. We forge into enemy territory. We are on our own.

The Spitfires can only go so far. The Thunderbolts and Lightnings can go pretty deep but they have limits with the existing drop tanks. There is supposed to be larger tanks coming to remedy this problem.

The word is that the Mustang is improved. After the British upgrades, it has become a different aircraft. It now possesses superior range and altitude.. The P-51 is supposed to be able to go anywhere we can. That's nice, but there isn't any here. We are alone on the deepest penetrations. We can defend ourselves only so much.

Penny doesn't sound right; something about the drone of the engines is off. The formation continues to the target as we start to lag behind.

Nick radios an abort. The number 2 engine has lost oil pressure. We cannot keep pace with a full bomb load. If we continue alone, we will be sitting ducks over enemy territory. Penny turns around for Old Buck.

By luck, we hook up with a squadron of P-38s. We got it made; Lightnings surround our lone bomber. Nothing can touch us now.

We arrive over Station #144 in an empty sky. The flaps are set before we turn on final approach. Nick flares Penny out to a smooth landing. We turn onto the ramp then taxi to our hardstand.

The mechanics get to work on the engine right away. Oil leaks, Waller Field has come back to haunt us. Penny is not going anywhere today. We are finished by 11:00 A.M. We sit here as the group flies the mission.

We are debriefed but we have nothing to report. No credit for another mission. I don't like this, it stinks. We can't even begin to tally the missions that will eventually get us back home. Thirty is the magic number and we still sit at zero.

We are told that there will be a weather front moving in. Old Buck will be socked in for a few days. We get to sulk for a while. We do all this flying and have nothing to show for it.

7. MISSIONS

Any man that volunteers for an aircrew has no idea what he is getting into.

Edmund M. Survilla

#1; Alerted; February 13th; Siracourt, France: Rocket installations. 2 A.M. wake up, get dressed, then head to the mess hall for breakfast. We grab a bite before we go to the briefing. All the crews for today's mission are here. We sit on benches facing a platform. A curtain covered map hangs on the wall behind it.

Our mission is revealed to us as the operations officer draws the curtain back. Today we strike Siracourt, France. We will go after the rocket installations. The planes will be loaded with 500 pound bombs for the strike. We are told our assigned speed and altitudes.

After we are briefed, we grab our flight bags and parachutes. We meet our officers at the bomber. Nick informs us that Burgess and Miller will no longer be flying with us.

Our new bombardier is Lieutenant Leslie Lee. He is a good-looking guy. He is a tall, dark haired fellow from Philadelphia, PA. He seems like a cool customer. Leslie likes a good time like everyone else.

Nick introduces us to our new navigator. He is Lieutenant Carl Powell. He is a little guy. We'll see if he is as good as Joe Miller. Carl seems really nice. He tells us in conversation that he is an avid shutterbug. After all the introductions, we return to the business of war.

Nick gives Penny a final walk around as we don our flight gear under Penny's wing. We position our chutes and gear at our posts. The ground crew is good. They have the extra ammunition laced in the feed track as requested.

The vets tell me to sit on my flak jacket. The reason for this is to protect my rear end from a FLAK burst going off beneath the plane. I would like to wear my parachute but it is too tight in the turret. That's just the way it is. I keep it near the escape hatch.

I wait until Penny is up and running, then I climb aboard. Luther exercises the propellers as Nick works the control surfaces. Everything is working properly, and we taxi out. Penny thunders down the runway and were off.

After the 453rd forms up, it turns for France. Spitfires come out to escort us. When the formation approaches the coast of France, they peel off. They are at the limit of their range. They are going home. The 453rd is on its own.

It is a nice, clear day, but it is cold. There isn't a German fighter to be seen in the crisp sky. So far so good, five minutes from target, Nick reports, "FLAK ahead."

The anti-aircraft barrage zeros in on our altitude. It looks like a big, black rain cloud, and we are going to go straight into it. I know this isn't good; planes go down in this stuff. The barrage is in our flight path. Nothing can be done. We have to fly through it.

The formation turns onto the Initial Point to begin the bomb run. The group doggedly holds steady on the preset course. A deviation in altitude or speed will throw the attack off target. We are sitting ducks locked in our bomb run. Oh my God, this is crazy. I didn't sign up for this.

The FLAK bursts are intense and accurate. "Lucky Penny" is rocked and pitched violently by near misses. What the hell is going on? I feel naked. There isn't anywhere to hide. Penny continues to get tagged by shrapnel. Nick and Luther keep the bomber steady as we approach the target.

Leslie reports, "Bomb bay doors opened." He waits; our bombardier will drop our bombs when the lead ship does. The anti-aircraft continue to hammer away. Penny is peppered with shrapnel. It sounds like somebody is standing outside of the plane with a hammer and punch driving holes into it. What the hell am I doing here?

The lead Liberator drops a marker bomb with its payload. This bomb leaves a trail of smoke when it falls. The whole formation can see it. This is the signal for the group to drop their bombs. CRUMPH, CRUMPH, the FLAK continues to torment us. Leslie reports, "Bombs away." He hits the switch to close the bomb bay doors.

I can't fight back against this. I just sit here in this turret. Oh God, don't let me get hit! Oh God, don't let…BANG. What the? Black smoke streams past the turret. What the fuck! The number four engine has taken a direct hit. The plane immediately starts a flat spin as it falls from the formation. Oh God, save me!

Penny starts to nose down, spinning out of control. The Liberator falls like a card that is tossed spinning through the air. Nick yells, "Bail out, bail out," as he hits the alarm. I do a back flip out of the turret. The moment I land in the fuselage, centrifugal force pins me to the side of the plane. This is insane. My parachute is right in front of me, and I can't even reach out for it.

I look forward to see Victor and Turwillger in the waist. They are hanging on to their guns for dear life. No expressions, their faces are covered with oxygen masks and goggles. They have their parachutes on but if they let go of their guns, the force of the spin will smash them against the side of the bomber. No doubt, Laddy is trapped in his little ball of a coffin.

What a way to go! We are all pinned where we stand, sit or lay. Penny has fallen thousands of feet already and we continue to spiral out of control. I tell myself I am going to be a prisoner of war. In reality, I am about to die.

There is a fight for life on the flight deck. Hansen screams, "Pull it out, come on guys, pull it out!" The spinning sensation begins to slow. Nick and Luther must have cut the throttles on the opposite engines. They have to be standing on the rudder pedals to correct the spin.

Our lives are in Nick and Luther's hands. The plane vibrates like a son-of-a-bitch. Hansen keeps yelling, "Pull it out, pull it out!" The spinning starts to slow but Penny noses into a steeper dive.

Finally, the spinning stops. If Nick and Luther can get us out of this dive maybe we can make it. Hansen continues to scream from his turret, "Come on, pull it out!" I listen to the scariest plea for salvation I have ever heard.

Slowly, Penny levels out. We have lost 12,000 feet, but our pilots have saved us from our spiral of death. Man, those bastards can fly this plane. I can't believe what just happened. No brown outs, but a few of us have pissed ourselves. Nick and Luther's hands shake from the ordeal. Their sweat covered faces stare into the sky in disbelief.

A voice cries out, "Thank God!" Somebody starts praying the Our Father out loud. Everybody joins the lone voice in prayer. Victor and Powell are Jewish but it does not matter. We all pray together. We are scared but, by God's merciful hand, we are still flying.

Laddy climbs out of his turret frightened by the ordeal. Everybody is stunned. Joe Craft tries to radio the group, but the Germans jam the airwaves. Nothing but loud squeal tones fill his headset.

Nick puts Penny on a course for home. The force of the dive blew the engine fire out but the plane vibrates badly. Nick can't feather the prop because the FLAK hit blew the propeller hub to junk. This propeller is going to windmill all the way home. I hope we don't toss a blade.

Our wounded ship vibrates but she still flies. I do not see any enemy fighters waiting to pounce on us either. The Germans must have thought we had it. Nick takes Penny as fast as she can handle. We hug the ground racing for the channel. There is not one enemy fighter to be seen. Come on now Penny, get us home.

We come limping into Old Buck. I'm sure the 453rd has written us off. Turwilliger fires a red flare before we come in on final approach. This indicates we have trouble. The crash trucks will be ready.

Luther lowers the landing gear. Unbelievably, they are in perfect working condition. Nick gingerly sets Penny down. The crash trucks follow us all the way to the hardstand. As soon as our Liberator stops, everybody scrambles out. Nick and Luther shut Penny down and get the hell out.

Our ground crew comes over excited to see us. They thought we were gone. They start joking, "What did you do to our plane?" We are so shaken we just walk away.

After we are debriefed, we go to the mess hall. Nobody is hungry. We sit at the table stupefied. After we play with our food for a while, we go to our shack. I lay in my bunk trying to pray myself to sleep. I pray for God to protect me.

My mortality dawns on me. I am scared, so scared. Oh God, help me. I am so scared my body is numb. Oh God, give me strength. I don't like this. I don't know if I can do this. I do not want to die. I try to live a good life. What will happen to my mom? What will I tell my mom? What will happen to my brother and sisters? What will happen when they hear I am dead? This is going to be a long war.

It was close today. All kinds of thoughts crowd my mind. I do not like playing this game. I am young and I want to live. I do not want to get in that plane again. I guess Penny is lucky though, she brought us home.

I am here. I am alive. Everybody on the plane made it. They all seem to be handling it O.K. What is my problem? Hey, if they can do it, I have to do it. God, just give me strength.

I contemplate my existence as I lay in my bunk. God, if I have to go, let it be quick. Let me be blown into a million pieces. Let me have my head blown off. I will never know it. I don't want to be trapped and ride it to the ground. I don't want to burn. I don't want to bail out and have my chute malfunction. Yes, I would become a prisoner of war to live. Would I trade a limb to live, maybe? If I have to go God, I beg you to make it quick. I pray my Rosary until I fall asleep.

#2; Alerted; February 24th; Gotha, Germany: Aircraft assembly plant. We are informed in the briefing that we are to strike the aircraft assembly plant in Gotha. We can expect heavy FLAK and fighters. P-47s then P-38s will rendezvous with us along the way. We are shown our route to and from the target.

Hey, this game is for keeps. I know this is dangerous, but man, oh man. That FLAK is nasty. A fighter escort is no defense against an anti-aircraft barrage.

We meticulously check our gear, this parachute better work. I hope these flak jackets are as good as advertised. I better get Nick and Luther their FLAK helmets. I'll set them on the flight deck. Let me take one last visit to the latrine before the truck arrives. Not much is said as we sling our gear on the back of the Duce and a Half. We take a sullen ride to our hardstand.

There's Penny. I do not even want to look at her, let

alone get in. The other guys are doing it even if it's grim determination that forces them. The false mask of bravado cannot hide their anxiety.

I arrange my gear next to the turret. The doors have been removed as I requested. Extra boxes of ammo have been laced into the feed tracks too. I have to give the ground crew credit. Penny is ready to fight.

We wait as Nick and Luther go through the preflight checklist. Soon enough we are taxiing out. We join the line of B-24s taxiing to the end of the runway. Boy, I hope we make it. Nick brings Penny onto the strip, and we're off.

Penny climbs to her place in the formation. We circle the base waiting for the rest of the group to form up. After the planes are Bunched, we turn for the enemy coast. I pray the Rosary as we cross the channel.

It is nice to have Thunderbolts riding along. They are big single engine brutes. When they reach their limit, the Lightnings will take over. Those bad boys will keep the Luftwaffe at bay.

In the clear blue sky, we cross into Fortress Europe. There is nothing in the way of the enemy to be seen, just the P-47s flying top cover. We rendezvous with the P-38s before the Jugs peel off. Boy, if the Germans are going to hit us, do it now.

Oh shit, there it is, FLAK. The P-38s fly above it. I don't know how the Germans can put so much anti-aircraft in the sky at one time. The formation wades into the barrage determined to strike Gotha.

The Lightnings have reached their limit; with a waggle of the wings, they are gone. They vanish into the distance. It feels lonely way up here; once again, we are on our own.

The formation finally emerges from the barrage unscathed. As we approach Gotha, FLAK fills the sky again. The Krauts are putting up a determined defense. CRUMPH, CRUMPH, black smoke from the bursts appear around us. You see it more than hear it. Penny is bounced and tossed, but Nick holds her steady.

Leslie takes control of the plane as we start the bomb run. He drops our bombs on the lead plane's mark. Penny lurches upward as her high explosive payload falls free. After passing over the target, the formation wheels on the heading that will take us back to Old Buck. Ok, we made it further than last time. Let's just get home.

It is a surprisingly clear day. It is easy to watch the bombs fall on the target. The strike walks across the aircraft factory, sweeping it under in a matter of seconds. The bombs wreak havoc on everything below. A dense black cloud rises from the assembly plant. It appears we have pounded it. Let's get the hell out of here.

We fly out of this barrage only to enter another of this menacing FLAK. There aren't any enemy fighters to be seen, but this anti-aircraft is vicious. I can do nothing. I just sweat it out in this turret. This stinks; I just sit here and wait to get blown out of the sky.

Wow, the FLAK claims a B-24. I wince as it dips a wing. The bomber begins a sickly tumbling corkscrew to earth. I don't know if anybody can get out. Wait, here comes a guy out of the rear escape hatch, two more emerge from the bomb bay. Here comes yet another. Yes, parachutes. It looks like four guys made it for sure.

The stricken bomber is too low to follow now. A few planes in the formation start to fall back, some are trailing smoke. Damn, how does that one stay in the air? The FLAK suddenly stops. That can only mean one thing.

There they are, fighters. They are little black specks on the horizon. They are German; our fighters can't go this deep into enemy territory. I report bandits at 5 o'clock. The specks grow larger against an ocean of blue. I have them in my sight, but I do not fire. They are way out of range.

The twin-engine Me-110s shadow the formation. They lay back and lob cannon shells at us. The rest of the German fighters fly parallel to the formation until they are out ahead. From there they turn into the bombers. This is a daring attack, head on. The Luftwaffe has learned the hard way that attacking under and behind an American bomber is a dangerous endeavor.

Me-109s and Fw-190s drive the attack home. They recklessly hurl themselves head long at the bombers. We do not face the teeth of this attack. Penny flies on the edge in the rear of the formation.

The Germans concentrate on the cockpits or engines of the lead aircraft. With guns blazing, the Krauts knife through the formation. They roll over and dive away in an instant. It happens so fast!

Some of them have yellow noses. These yellow-nosed fighters are known as the Abbeville Kids. They are a crack German group. We call them the Yellow Nosed Bastards. After the Kraut fighters dive out of range, they prepare for another pass.

The Germans tear through the formation again. The guys calmly report where the fighters are coming from. They flash by Penny before they dive away. Victor yells out, "I got one!" Two German fighters rush by with one smoking. There are planes falling and diving everywhere. Crazily scribbled contrails streak across the sky.

The bombers tuck in tight. This box formation gives interlocking fields of fire. I track my targets careful not to be wild. I let loose short bursts as Krauts streak past.

If you are shooting at a plane and a closer target presents itself, always go after that aircraft. Penny vibrates from her firing guns. You can feel the guns firing more than you hear them. You can tell who is firing by the vibrations you feel.

Hansen reports, "Bandits coming in again." You can't miss the yellow noses. Three keep coming through the formation. The lead Kraut does not fire. The other two fighters rollout and dive away.

The lone Me-109 keeps coming. Nick yells out, "You got one coming; you got one coming down your side!" I know Nick is talking to me. I know what he means. Nick yells again, "Here he comes, down your side!"

The lethal confrontation is over in an instant, but in my mind's eye, it happens in slow motion. I spin the turret to the right until it hits its stop. The fighter passes just under Penny's wing tip. My God, this guy is close. The pilot isn't even wearing his oxygen mask. He has a dark colored beard. He looks at me as he streaks by.

I say to myself, "I'm going to get you." By pure chance, I have the guns pointed in the right direction. As soon as I see the yellow nose, I let loose. At point blank the .50 calibers spit out a flat staccato of lead. Half-inch slugs fly through the air. Hits appear right behind the spinner of the Me-109. The bullets track in a straight line from the nose to the cockpit.

The pilot suddenly bolts up, turns sideways, and then slumps forward in his harness. The Hun goes into a smoke trailing power dive that he never recovers from. This guy is dead. I sawed him in half.

The air is charged with excitement. I blurt out, "I got him, I got him!" Nick excitedly replies, "That Yellow Nosed Bastard waved at me when he went by!" Nick exclaims, "I think he was an ace. I saw the markings on his tail."

Our escorts finally drive the Krauts off. In the distance, a classic dogfight takes place. Two fighters are locked in a deadly turn. One plane is trying to get inside the other to deliver the kill. Thank God for our fighters.

The formation leaves the melee behind as we continue our journey home. Penny pulls us through again. Our remaining escorts take us over the channel to East Anglia.

The group transitions into a holding pattern above our base. We fly circuits until it is our turn to land. Luther sets the flaps as we turn on final approach. The landing gear is lowered, and Nick brings a victorious Penny in.

Excitement fills the air as we emerge from under the plane. I am thrilled over my kill. I have destroyed my enemy. Major Stewart drives out to meet the officers. He yells out, "How did it go, Black Fury?" I reply, "O.K. sir, I got myself a Tin Can Bastard, Me-109." Major Stewart gives me a smile and thumbs up as he drives by.

The Duce and Half takes us to debriefing. The officers there always have a shot of brandy waiting. I knock one back. "Would you like another?" I am asked. "Sure," I reply. "Well, you can't," he tells me. "Tell me what happened and what you saw." I tell the interrogation officer about the anti-aircraft and my fighter kill. I describe the head on attacks and bomber losses. After I answer all I am asked,

Laddy takes his turn.

We are confident as we go to the mess hall. The cooks treat us well. They always prepare a good meal for the aircrews. Satisfied, we go to our barracks.

I feel pretty good. I can live through this. I even got a Me-109. You bet your ass if he could have got me, he would have. Penny the dog will sleep with us tonight. I say my prayers before I hit the rack.

The gun camera footage comes back. The film doesn't lie. I blasted that Me-109. The ground crew paints our second bomb on the plane along with the two kills. The nineteen-year-old kid of the crew gets Penny her first kill. Victor knocked one down, and I got one too.

(Note: February 20th to the 26th, 1944, will be known as Big Week. These were the first extensive raids carried out by the 8th Air Force. These raids were designed to destroy the German aircraft industry.)

A little stand down time has come our way. The 453rd has been taking loses and there isn't any maximum efforts to be flown. Penny's crew gets to take a break.

Finally, I can take a shower. When you're on alert and flying, there is no time, and you are too tired to clean up. To be honest, you really don't care. It is the last thing on your mind. A person really smells after a few days, but nobody notices because everybody stinks.

After everybody is cleaned up, we are issued passes and hop a ride into town. Our main objective is booze and women. We wet our whistles at the first pub we come across.

Most of the civilians are cordial and fun to be around. Some of the snobby, upper class people look down at us with disapproval. Who cares, we are here to chase girls. There is always the chance an airman could have a nice place to spend the night. There is the likelihood of some good food and drink for the girls. The odds of getting some action is always a possibility.

There are all kinds of people in the pub, servicemen and civilians. There is the usual bravado and wise cracking from the other branches of the service. It is all in fun. The locals proudly tell us to give Hitler hell.

We wind up talking with a B-17 crew. The first joke is always the same. I would rather see my sister in a whorehouse than in a B-17. It is all lighthearted for we all share the same fate.

The drinks start to flow, and the women look good. They are looking for companionship, too. They have lost husbands or lovers to the enemy. Actually, they are looking for men, period. Britain has been fighting since 1939 and many young English men are fighting or dead.

A guy usually buys a woman a few drinks in hopes of breaking the ice. If the objective is met, a guy would take her out for a roll in the grass. Yet another form of attack is to duck your date into an alley. You lean her against a wall, pull her panties down and drive it home. I like to bend them over a mailbox. If a guy plays his cards right, he could get more than one jump a night.

When the hell raising and womanizing is over, a guy can get a hotel room or stay as a guest in a family's home. It feels good to lay your head down in a real bed. It is even better to feel a female body laying next to you.

Some of the guys develop relationships, content with one girl. Other guys have their fun then go hunting for more. As the saying goes, "Eat, drink and be merry, for tomorrow may never come."

#3; Alerted; February 25th; Furth, Germany: Aircraft factory. The orderly awakens us at 2:00 A.M. Of course, Laddy and I are goofing off as we wait for the briefing to begin. Most everybody gabs or smart mouths with each other.

As soon as the operations officer enters, all of that stops. We are told to sit down. Everybody pays attention now. The officer unveils the map to show us our target. This mission should take about eight hours. We are told to expect heavy FLAK and fighters. We are told our assigned altitudes, what type of bombs will be used and so forth.

After the briefing, the guys make one last visit to the latrine. Everybody makes sure they have their equipment before we hop on the truck. We ride down the flight line to our bomber. The crew gathers in the darkness under Penny's wing. Nick gives us our final instructions.

"Come on, Tiger!" we call out to Powell. He lugs all of his charts, maps and equipment into the bomb bay. We grab him and boost him up into the plane. Our shutterbug is an alright guy. He has taken numerous pictures of the crew already. He most certainly is a camera hound.

Up on the flight deck, Nick and Luther go down the preflight checklist. Nick un-cages the gyros before he continues. Batteries, fuel settings, cowl flaps. magnetos, lean, rich mixtures, etc. After each item, Luther checks it off. The engines have been turned and all is set.

I go back outside to stand watch as the engines are started. Nick hangs his head out the window and yells, "Clear on two." The propeller starts spinning. Moments later, the cylinders start to catch. The engines belch puffs of white smoke until all the cylinders are firing.

The inboard engines are always started first. If an outboard engine were to be started first, a person would have to contend with the spinning propeller of the outboard engine on the way to a troublesome inboard engine.

Luther repeats the same process on his side of the plane until all the engines are running. Nick waits for the cylinder heads get to temperature before he runs the engines up. The gauges checkout, all is fine. As soon as I climb aboard, the bomb bay doors are closed behind me.

Nick gets Penny rolling forward a little before he turns onto the taxi ramp. This is done to get the nose wheel straight. If it is cocked, it may collapse while trying to turn off the pad. Penny falls into her place in this impressive line of bombers. The procession taxis to the end of the strip. The control tower signals go with the firing of a flare.

The 453rd begins to take to the skies once again. I wonder what is going to happen this time.

I start my trek aft as the formation crosses the channel. I stop in the bomb bay to perform another duty of mine. This job is to pull the safety pins from the bombs.

A bomb has a small propeller on the front of it. This propeller spins when the bomb starts to fall. The spinning action arms it. The safety pin keeps the propeller from turning when the bomb is being handled. When I pull the pins, I hang on to them just in case. You never know what could happen. I have had to put them back in the bombs three times already.

As I continue to the tail, I watch Victor and Turwilliger help Laddy into his turret. Laddy slides in the ball then Victor closes the hatch. Laddy locks the latch from inside. With a thumbs up he signals all is ready. The ball turret is lowered out of the well to hang under Penny. That's a hell of a thing. No thanks, I'll take the tail.

As soon as I settle on my seat, I watch a Liberator make a banking turn for home. Obviously, this guy is aborting. Five minutes later two more bombers turn away. These are obvious aborts also. What's going on? Do these guys know something we don't?

The formation continues to the target. Carter holds his position on our wing in a turbulent sky. Our escorts pull broken contrails above as another B-24 in our box turns away. There appears to be nothing wrong with any of the aborting bombers. After some speculation, the crew concurs that something is up.

Luther cynically comments, "Abort early and avoid the rush." I jokingly think to myself, "Do the Krauts have some kind of secret weapon we don't know about?" The last of the aborting Liberators turn for home as we reach the enemy coast.

CRUMPH, CRUMPH, here we go again. Boy, I hate this stuff. We aren't even over the target yet. I really hate playing with my life. The black cloud of FLAK comes into view as we enter it. It suddenly appears around me. I never get to see it coming. Once again, Penny is getting pelted. At least there are no fighters. At the rate this FLAK is coming up, we may never see a German fighter.

The formation begins to pull contrails. I don't like this either. I can't get a good view of my surroundings. No matter, fighters are not the problem now, the FLAK is.

Shit, anti-aircraft claims another B-24. This bomber falls back, slowly losing altitude. Flames leap from a burning inboard engine. They lap at the mangled stabilizer. The pilot is desperately fighting to keep his bomber up. There they go, the crew starts bailing out. They appear as little black specks. Six guys fall free, then two more. I can't see what's going on anymore. The contrails and FLAK obscure my view of this dying plane.

They will become prisoners of war. I am glad it is not me. I hear the peasants are beating aircrews to death when they land. Rakes, shovels, it doesn't matter. They bludgeon their tormentors from the sky viciously. I have my pistol, if I have to bail out, I will shoot everybody I can and save the last bullet for myself.

FLASH, pieces of plane explode everywhere. They tumble back in the slipstream. Wow, that was bright! Holy smoke, it takes a moment for the brain to register what the eyes just saw.

Our opposite wing man just took a direct hit. An 88mm shell must have found its mark in the bomb bay. Incredible, one moment he is on our wing, the next a sheet of fire and pieces of plane are falling from the sky. One second I am watching the waist gunner, the next he is gone. My stomach knots as I break into a cold sweat.

A section of wing with engines still turning hangs in the sky. It tries to pull a non-existent plane into the heavens. The flight deck floor tumbles away with the remains of the pilots still strapped in their seats. What a weird sight! Wing tips and ailerons flutter away like leaves. Propellers, wheels and engines arc across the sky.

The tail section falls earthward intact. It corkscrews and tumbles crazily with the tail gunner in it. If he is alive, he's taking the ride. Yes, I can see some of the bodies that were men flying next to me moments ago. They just fall away. I don't believe it; in an instant a plane is gone. I hate the Krauts. I hope we tear this target to pieces.

The formation turns on to the I.P. Come hell or high water, we are committed to the run. The bombers fly straight and level to the target. The lead plane drops its bombs and the group follows. Our deadly payload is on its way. We turn for home before the bombs hit the ground.

There is no relief from this son-of-a-bitchin FLAK. Cowering on my seat is all I can do as the barrage intensifies. I wish we could fly our own course out of this deadly trap, no can do. The lead bomber instructs the group to loosen up. This is crazy! All I can do is sweat this baby out.

The anti-aircraft dogs us all the way to the coast. Spitfires pick us up and escort us across the channel. The 453rd turns for East Anglia as the Spitfires go their own way.

Once over Old Buck, Nick puts Penny into a racetrack pattern. Our pilot flies circuits until it is our turn to land. With a squeal of the tires, Nick brings the bomber in. We taxi down the ramp to our hardstand. The mighty Pratt & Whitney's are shut down before we exit the plane. Well, Penny has carried us home once again.

The truck takes us down the line to the debriefing. We answer all the questions we are asked. After we finish, we proceed to the mess hall. We are informed, of the 24 bombers that were in the raid, 12 had aborted. We go to our shack to get some needed shuteye.

I get out my big map of Europe and trace the path of this raid. I will do this for every mission. Who knows, maybe I will make it. Maybe I'll get married and have kids someday. This map will be a keepsake. I get my prayer book out and read my pages. I am tired and saddened. I don't like what I saw today.

February 28th we are flying a practice mission, I really hate this. We will play war today. Everybody has to go, fully armed. Then again, it is a necessary evil; we get new crews coming all the time. These guys have to see how it's done. I certainly don't need a trigger happy replacement shooting at me. I don't need a new pilot sticking a wing in my turret. So be it, we will fly around England.

The world is really different at 28,000 feet. If a person did not have good eyes, they wouldn't even see us from the ground. It's those contrails that give us away. They broadcast where you are. That's enough of that, this practicing stinks. There isn't any credit for flying and who knows what could happen. We land and get lost.

#4; Alerted; March 5th; Cazaux, France: Airdrome. Due to the weather, there has only been one mission flown in the past eight days. This is good; the 453rd has been getting hammered. These last couples of days have been nice. If you don't fly, you don't die.

Not today, we are back in the fight. At least we aren't going deep into enemy territory. I just don't like sweating my life every time I climb into Penny. We will destroy an airstrip. We will walk a carpet of bombs the length of the target area. After we gather our gear, we are trucked out to the plane.

We stand on frozen ground as we put on our flight gear. I tell myself I am dead. This is the only way I can bring myself to climb into the bomber. If I am already dead, it doesn't matter. We are reminded; harnesses are to be worn at all times while in the plane. We have been issued heated suits, let's see how they work. It would be nice to not freeze your ass off up there for once.

Nick and Luther go through the checklist. After the throttles are set, Nick hangs his head out the window and yells, "Clear on two." The starter cranks the propeller around a few times until the cylinders start to catch. The engine stumbles and misses until all the cylinders are firing. The motor settles into a smooth idle. This is repeated on the remaining engines until all four are turning. The engines are run up, all checks good. They are put back to idle before we taxi out.

Penny takes us down the ramp to the end of the runway. Nick swings our B-24 onto the strip and guns the throttles. The four engines surge to life. They pull Penny down the runway and carry us into the sky. Penny climbs to join the circling bombers. We take our assigned position on the right edge of a formation.

The group's combat boxes look good as we enter France. CRUMPH, here we go again. The Krauts aren't throwing up too much FLAK, but it only takes one well placed shot. I'll just have to sit here and wait to get hit. I will do my job and search the sky.

Nick has discovered a new maneuver. Some veteran must have told him about it. "Lucky Penny" begins to zig-zag on the edge of the element.

When a bracket of FLAK comes up in front of us, Nick slides Penny to either side of it. When the next bracket of FLAK comes up, it is where we would have been if we were flying straight. Nick slides Penny back before the following bracket comes up in the position we had just vacated, pretty nifty.

No more of that when we approach the I.P. Nick lines Penny up for the bomb run then gives control to Leslie. Leslie checks for correct speed and altitude. We are dropping ... Hey, what the hell is going on?

I can't breathe! I am not getting any oxygen. I look around the turret. What the hell is wrong now? With a tug, the oxygen hose moves freely. The hose is cut clean in half. Son-of-a-bitchin FLAK. I grab the emergency oxygen bottle and take a breath. Christ all mighty, this thing is empty too!

I report my situation to Nick, at least the intercom still works. Nick tells me, "Stay put. After the bomb run we will drop down." I reply, "You better not. I can see a whole gaggle of German fighters below just waiting to pounce." Nick tells me, "O.K, just sit still and breathe easy."

That is what I do. I calmly sit on my little seat as the formation delivers its bombs. I breathe as shallow as I can. There is absolutely no reason I should be conscious, but I am. I am being watched over.

Halfway back home, the skies look clear enough for me to go for a different oxygen bottle. I stay on station until we get below 10,000 feet. The formation finally crosses into Jolly Ole England.

The 453rd comes in over Norfolk County. We circle Old Buck until it is our turn to land. Ten minutes later, Nick brings Penny in. We rollout to the end of the runway and taxi our bomber to her hardstand. We slowly emerge from under our faithful Liberator.

Before I get my gear off, I hunt down the ground crew. I find the culprit and raise hell about the empty oxygen bottle. Nick tells the offending ground crew member, "This will not happen again." The message is understood.

I am assured it will not happen again. We are trucked to debriefing where we relay the events of today's mission. After everybody is interrogated, we head to the mess hall for a good hot cup of coffee.

We learn we will be losing Penny for awhile. She will be upgraded. Penny will be getting armor plates in the cockpit area. She will be getting supercharger upgrades and so forth. We will be equipped like the new B-24 models. We will be flying a different plane until she is refurbished. We will fly the plane of a crew that is on leave.

#5; Alerted; March 6th; Berlin, Germany: This is it, everybody is alerted. The operations officer tells us, "It's the big one!" The raid will not be called off this time.

A few bombers did not get the recall three days ago. They went on and bombed Berlin anyway. There will not be an abort this time. Holy smokes, we are going to bomb Hitler's house!   He wants war; he is going to get war.

This is a maximum effort. All the heavy bomb groups are going. The heavy bomb groups out of Italy will be in on this also. The attack will come from the west and south. All of the bombers will converge on Berlin, impressive.

Everybody wants to fly this one. The group C.O. Col. Miller, Col. Dowda, Major Hubbard and Major Stewart are going, to name a few. Just about every fighter group will be in on this one too.

With the new drop tanks, the P-38s and P-47s can make it all the way to Berlin, if they do not run into any action along the way. That's O.K. with me boys! Get them Krauts anytime you can.

The new Mustangs have arrived a couple of weeks ago. I hear they are hot birds. With the new drop tanks, they are supposed to go a long way. Berlin is supposed to be no problem. They say the Mustangs can linger with the new tanks. Well, we will need them. I am sure Hitler will be throwing up everything he has.

We take the utmost care getting ready for this mission. It's an awkward kind of feeling. It is exhilarating knowing we are going to hit Berlin, yet we are scared as ever. Death is always looking over your shoulder. You cannot shake it off. The dark angel is always riding along.

We pile on the back of the truck that takes us out to the planes. We will not be flying Penny today. She is being refurbished. We ride out to the hardstand of the "Paper Doll," instead. I hope she is a good plane. Treat us right baby.

The "Paper Doll" is another original bomber of the 453rd. She is olive drab and gray also. Painted under the cockpit is a beautiful girl leaning forward with her arms out. She wears a one-piece bikini. Between the nose and the girl the name" Paper Doll" is painted in white letters.

The ground crew of the "Paper Doll" briefs Nick and Luther. Our pilots are informed about this Liberator's idiosyncrasies. The ground crew tells us to take care of their plane. After the preflight checklist, the "Paper Doll" is fired up and taxied out.

We fall into line with every bomber that can fly. The ramps are full of idling B-24s waiting to go. The "Paper Doll" slowly moves forward until it is our turn to takeoff. Without stopping, we turn onto the runway. With a push of the throttles, the "Paper Doll" jumps into the sky.

Aircraft of the surrounding bomb groups form up on their rally ships as they circle their airbases. We spot that green and yellow checkered monstrosity of a plane that is our rally ship. The 453rd falls in behind it. "Wham Bam" leads us to our place in this massive bomber stream.

The bombers stretch as far as I can see. It's not a bomber stream in the strictest sense. A true bomber stream is individual aircraft lined up in single file to attack a target. The British use this method when attacking cities. Each bomber arrives over the target separately stretching the raid over a prolonged period of time. It is a method of terror warfare.

This raid is so big that formations of bomb groups get in line behind each other. Each group is a segment of the stream. Each group would represent a single aircraft in a true bomber stream. The scale of the attack is enormous.

The bomb groups out of the south link up with the bombers out of England en route. The stream grows massive in size. Cripes, I have never seen so many planes at once. It looks like flocks of birds going south for the winter. There has to be a thousand bombers up here. Who knows what the bomb tonnage is?

There is no doubt; this is a show of force. We are going to punish Berlin. I wonder what this stream looks like from the ground. It must be a hell of a sight. The people of England had to be watching planes fly out for hours. I wonder what this sounds like from the ground.

The British really want a piece of this action. Their patrolling Spitfires go with the stream as far as they can then turn back. Squadrons of P-38s, P-47s and P-51s cruise with the bombers. Some fly top cover while others roam out ahead of this massive strike force. Others take up station at given points in the stream.

It is impossible to cover the whole length of this train in the sky. The fighters fly where they think it works best for their strategy. I don't know how the Krauts could get past them. I like this, my chances seem pretty good. Let's get to Berlin, give it to Hitler and get out.

There it is, FLAK. My stomach knots up again. This is no way to live. I am sick with fear and I am sick and tired of being sick with fear. The fighters cannot do a thing about the FLAK. We are just part of this long stream that must go through the black curtains of anti-aircraft, thrown up in front of us.

The Germans pick their battles; they tear into bombers 30 miles back. Free-for-alls erupt all over the sky. Bombers fall, from FLAK or fighters, in the melees that erupt along the length bomber stream.

Fighters criss-cross the sky locked in aerial combat. Crashed aircraft and parachutes make a visible path that the bombers can follow right to Berlin. I just sit and wait to get killed as the Paper Doll is tossed about. No enemy fighters here but we run into intense FLAK that shudders the plane. CRUMPH, that one was close!

Moments later, Nick calls me forward to check on the nose. I grab a portable oxygen bottle and I am on my way. Turwilliger gives me a quick glance in passing. He returns to searching the skies with Victor for enemy fighters. Laddy spins in his turret below as I skirt the well.

Next, it's into the bomb bay. The bombs hang poised for action. They will soon rain destruction on Berlin.

As I enter the radio compartment, Joe Craft gives me a look. He has it the worst. He doesn't have a gun to man. He just sits there. He gestures," What is going on?" I give him the universal shrug of the shoulders. Hansen spins his turret searching for the enemy as I reach Nick and Luther.

With a puzzled look on his face, Nick tells me, "Check on Powell." A quick duck under the flight deck takes me to the nose. Leslie gestures at Powell. There appears to be nothing wrong with him but he is pale and really spooked. Our navigator sits babbling at his table. Carl continually repeats, "Hitler knows I'm here. He knows I'm a Jew. Hitler knows I'm here. He knows I'm a Jew."

Leslie points to the Astro-Dome. It is shattered. A FLAK burst went off directly in front and above the "Paper Doll". A piece of shrapnel went through the navigational dome just missing Powell's head. It continued to the flight deck where it hit Nick's rudder pedal. The hot piece of steel then knocked the heel off of Nick's boot. Luckily, nobody was hurt.

I report the situation to Nick. I am told to bring Powell to the flight deck. He babbles incoherently as I urge him to the cockpit. He sits behind the pilots, truly shaken.

This near miss may have broken him. Each man is informed what happened as I return to my turret. We continue to be tormented by FLAK, but there isn't a single enemy fighter to be seen.

Berlin's punishment can clearly be seen from miles away. The city is an inferno. Bombs continue to rain down on a devastated metropolis. I know it isn't possible, but I swear I just saw a stove top come up in that explosion. Nothing escapes destruction, Berlin is being laid waste, and I do not care.

I hope we bomb those bastards back into the Stone Age. Leslie drops our bombs on the lead bomber's signal. Here you go Adolf and there is a lot more to come.

Our payload delivered, we need only to follow the bombers ahead of us home. Remarkably, we fly the return leg as the remainder of the stream drives home the attack. Just about every American heavy bomber in theater converges on Berlin.

I watch the capitol of Hitler's Germany fade in the distance. The aerial pounding continues, the heart of the city will be reduced to rubble. To hell with you dirty rat, bastard Krauts. The 453rd lives up to its motto, Attack and Destroy. Welcome to the war, Adolph.

Our part of the stream is not harassed the rest of the way home. The "Paper Doll" has pulled us through. We have done our part in this spectacular daylight raid.

We fly a holding pattern over Old Buck until it's our turn to land. After a few circuits, Nick flares the Doll out as he gently sets her down. We taxi to her hardstand and shut her down.

Our ground crew has waited with the "Paper Doll's" for our return. They all want to make sure we made it. They gather around listening intently as we give an account of this incredible daylight raid. Some guys shake their heads in disbelief when they are told the size of it. Other guys stand there picturing the mission in their minds.

The 453rd lost four planes today; some bomb groups were torn to shreds. There was a report of a whole B-17 group being wiped out, save the lead bomber. When the pilot told the tail gunner to check on the rest of the group, the tail gunner replied, "Where is it?" There was nothing there, only an empty sky. The 109s and 110s launched a vicious assault on that particular section of the stream.

The Luftwaffe sent fighters up to keep our escorts occupied while the main attacks tore into sections of the bomber stream. The Krauts attacked until they exhausted their ammo. They landed and rearmed, only to attack a different segment of the massive raid.

After debriefing, we grab a bite. An exhausted crew crawls to the barracks. I grab the doll and mark this mission on him. I trace the path to Berlin on my map. Before I crash into my rack, I put another entry into my diary. Maybe I'll get lucky and dream of home.

Joe Craft grumbles, "Turn off the light." He is ignored. Another request gets the same result. Agitated, Joe pulls his .45 pistol. POW, POW, POW, he shoots the light out. Shattered glass showers to the floor.

Everybody is awake now. Angry voices split the darkness. "What the hell? Are you goofy or something?" "What the hell is wrong with you?" "What are you nuts?" George Neamy yells, "You're going to clean this mess up and you are fixing those holes in the roof. If you think I am kidding, I will report your ass." With the excitement over, everybody's ire subsides. The sound of the burning wood in the stove carries me off to sleep.

#6; Alerted; March 8th; Berlin, Germany: We will hammer Berlin again. Hitler wants war; well, he will be getting it again. We report for the briefing. We are informed it will be another bomber stream like before. There is nothing strategic about this attack. We are bombing Berlin to send a message. This is all about breaking the will of the enemy. I leave the briefing wondering if the 453rd will be the group caught in the Luftwaffe meat grinder today.

After we grab our gear, we truck out to the Paper Doll. She pulled us through once; I hope she can do it again. After we perform our preflight rituals, Powell is boosted into the plane with maps and charts in tow. I make sure extra ammo is laced into the guns. Everybody sets their FLAK helmets and parachutes in the proper places. Crew 41 prepares to fight.

Nick and Luther do their visual inspection of the "Paper Doll". They walk around the B-24 looking for any obvious problems. Satisfied, they climb aboard to start the preflight checklist. Soon enough the Liberator roars to life. We taxi onto the ramp and join the planes that are going to hit Berlin again.

It is impressive sitting among this idling armada. Nick slowly moves down the ramp waiting his turn to take flight. Once at the head of the runway, Nick swings the Doll onto the strip. With the throttles cracked wide open, she carries us into the wild blue.

Nick takes his place on the edge of the upper element. The replacement crews fly in the middle of the group. The hardened crews surround them until they get a couple missions under their belts.

The 453rd follows "Wham Bam" to its assigned place in this second massive bomber stream. The escorts take up station as we journey to Berlin. Once again, bombers can be seen to the horizon. What an imposing sight.

The anti-aircraft begins tormenting us as soon as we penetrate enemy territory. It is no secret where we are going. A black cloud of FLAK begins to form in the distance. Another group, in the stream, is taking a vicious beating. They can have it.

The "Paper Doll" goes haywire as soon as we enter Germany. She isn't pulling good manifold pressure. Two superchargers are gone. Two engines are heating up and we are losing oil pressure. It is imperative to our safety that we stay with the stream. Nick and Luther try coaxing the Liberator along. Our ailing B-24 starts to lag behind. Nick reluctantly drops out of the stream. The bombers continue above us in a relentless march to Berlin.

We can't have our asses hanging in the wind; a straggler will be blown out of the sky. If the Krauts see us, we are done. They will hop on us like a pack of wolves.

We are better off turning back; Nick has Joe Craft radio an abort. We descend to 5,000 feet leaving the stream behind. The "Paper Doll" performs well in the heavier air. There is no need for the superchargers at this altitude; the bomber runs fine.

It's kind of spooky flying alone in enemy territory. The crew is tense as we cruise through an empty sky. Eyes are peeled waiting for an enemy that never appears. The Germans are concentrating on the defense of Berlin. We fly over the French countryside ignored.

Nick instructs Powell to find a target of opportunity as we scurry home. After mulling through his charts, Powell gives Nick a heading for a rail junction and airfield. Nick chooses the depot. Moments later, Nick banks the bomber onto the course mapped out by our navigator.

We begin our run on the station. Leslie gets in the nose turret in preparation for the aerial assault. We will be coming in low and fast. He will use the turret gun sight instead of the bombsight for the attack.

The top-secret Norden bombsight is designed for high altitude bombing. This tool of war is a mechanical wonder that works in conjunction with the autopilot. It calculates altitude, speed and wind drift automatically. It has brought accuracy to high altitude bombing. Although all the bombers are equipped with one, the standard practice is to follow the lead bomber's signal.

There is no need for the Norden bombsight down here. Powell's course has put us on a set of train tracks that lead us to the depot. Nick simply follows the rails to the target. The "Paper Doll" hurls down the tracks like a runaway locomotive. Nick turns on the I.P. He nudges the controls until the depot is in Leslie's gun sight.

When Leslie guesstimates the correct distance, he releases the Doll's deadly payload. The 500-pound bombs are salvoed on the target. I have the best seat in the house as we thunder over the depot. The high explosives rain on the objective. They crash through the roof of the depot. KABLAM, in a brilliant flash the roof is blasted 300 feet into the air. It breaks into millions of pieces before it showers to the ground.

I excitedly report, "Holy shit, we just blew the roof off of that building!" The crew erupts into laughter and hooting. Leslie shouts out, "Let's go around again." Everybody laughs in agreement. Nick, in his better judgment, tells us, "No, we better not." The Paper Doll leaves the shattered remains of a building and twisted rails in her wake.

The Liberator continues to perform well at low altitude. Nick rides the B-24 hard making a beeline for home. We race back to England at over 300 miles per hour. There isn't any FLAK or German fighter to be seen as we haul ass across the channel. The "Paper Doll" is brought into Old Buck hours before the group returns.

Nick taxis off the ramp to the Doll's hardstand. The ground crew is relieved to see us alive and well. We emerge from the bomb bay elated. We laugh about our one plane air strike over a smoke.

When did the crew start smoking? Nick and Luther inform the ground crew of the planes problems. They get to work on it immediately. After we get out of our gear, the truck takes us to debriefing.

The interrogators ask us, "What happened?" We tell the officers about the engine troubles that caused our abort. We recount our one plane raid on the depot. We are told we did a good job. We pulled off a daring single-handed strike, and made it home. We wander off to the mess hall for a hearty meal.

We start our R&R tomorrow. It feels good to know we will not have to fly for a couple of days. We are informed we will receive the Air Medal for these two raids. We had to go to Berlin to earn it. I got to see Berlin before I get to see London. Laddy brings the dog over from the officer's barracks. Penny will sleep with us tonight. He takes his favorite place by the stove.

(Note: The strategic objective of the Berlin raids was to gain air superiority. Only known to the high command, the bombers were no more than decoys. Their purpose was to draw the Luftwaffe into the sky so Allied Fighter Command could force them into combat. The intent was to deal crippling blows to the Luftwaffe. Further cities would be attacked in execution of this strategy.)

March 12th, laundry run. The M.P. challenges Joe Craft, Laddy and me at the gate. It is the same thing every time. He asks, "Where are your uniforms? You can't leave the base without proper dress." We give the same reply every time, "Sorry, Mack, leather jackets are proper dress for the Air Corps."

Our leather jackets do look good; they broadcast what we do. We have our plane's name painted on them, most crews do. The jacket is a status symbol. Everybody knows the dangerous job associated with a decorated leather jacket. We get no more than a disapproving shake of the head as the M.P. lets us pass.

The local kids gathered at the base fence salute us as we pass. We answer in kind. The kids look up to us. We are heroes, gallant figures. They marvel at the B-24s, and they know the names of every single plane.

Occasionally, the ground crews invite the kids to the hardstands. It is against regulations but it is overlooked. The children take great pride in the privilege of being able to watch the bombers as they are repaired or serviced.

Sometimes when the youngsters are by the planes, they would ask, "Did you get any Jerries?" They wait wide-eyed for an answer. With a mean look, you tell them, "Yeah, we gave it to Hitler." They excitedly reply, "Good job, Yank! Give it to Hitler!" They want to hear from us. It is a great honor to talk to us. They are a curious bunch but they never get in the way.

After school, there is always a bunch of them gathered by the fence at the end of the runway. They look for their favorite plane, hoping it made it back. The children wave like mad when a plane comes in. Of course, when you see them, you wave back. We have a fan club and we like it.

We take a walk down the road to the little house just beyond the end of the base. It is modest, the English don't have much. They have been at war for a while now. There is a woman there that does our laundry. She lives there with her little boy.

What a nice person she is. I don't know if her husband is off to war or dead. I don't ask. She stays at home and raises her son. He is a good little kid. He is always thrilled to see us. She does our wash and we give her C-rations or chocolate in return.

She tells us how she counts the planes when they return from a mission. She admits she sometimes cries at the thought of us young men not coming back. She tells us, "Every time you boys takeoff, I say a prayer for you." Her words are heartfelt, and we thank her for such kind thoughts. We leave our laundry with some rations and chocolate for the boy.

We return to Old Buck in time for mail call. It is always something to look forward to. Helen writes me all the time. She sent me another Rosary. She also sent me a pink ribbon to remind me of her. I think I'll pin it to my cap. Boy she is a good girl. She must really care about me.

On my letters to Helen, I put a capital letter in the corner of each envelope. This is over looked by the sensors. I do this until I spell out a target we have bombed. If she stacks her letters in order it will spell out the name of a target, B-E-R-L-I-N, for example.

Everybody shares the food or candy they get from home. Crew 41 is its own family. The Carter crew is our extended family. The guys you met when you enlisted are your friends.

A guy doesn't bother much with others outside of these circles. There are two reasons. First of all, you don't see other guys much unless you are at a briefing or the mess hall. The second reason is it hurts too much when a friendly face disappears.

I can still see that blonde haired guy I would run into at

the mess hall. He was killed about a week ago. He was a radio operator. He was a handsome guy. He was such a nice guy. He was shot down and I can't even remember his name. I know this; instead of plowing into some field in Germany, I would rather die in my plane and have it carry me home.

By noon, we hitch a ride to Attleboro. From there we ride the train to London. We will try to be tourists, but we will undoubtedly find our way to a bar.

Two hours later, we arrive at Piccadilly Circus; it is just like Time Square in New York. The place bustles with activity as civilians and service personnel go about their lives. We wander the streets before we hit the pubs.

Our sightseeing takes us to a bombed out section of London. So this is what the results of an air raid look like. Some of the city blocks are just piles of rubble. There are paths cleared where the streets used to be. Some buildings are just skeletons. No floors, roofs or anything. They are no more than five story brick faces. Other buildings are ripped opened. You can see the different rooms, the colors they are painted and all the furniture.

Men work diligently recovering bodies or demolishing buildings. A Bobby warns us to stay back. "You cannot go any further. There is a live bomb being defused down the street." We do not want any part of that and make our way back to Piccadilly Circus.

We enter the door of the first pub we see. As soon as I walk in, a serviceman, I have never seen before, walks up to me and punches me right between the eyes. There is utterly no rhyme or reason. Jesus Christ, I'm bleeding too.

Before I could gather my senses, my attacker runs out the door. I am pissed but he is gone. Surprised, Joe and Laddy calm me down. I grab a drink, grumbling how I would like to kill that son-of-a-bitch. My leave in London starts with a punch right between the eyes.

We order the first round of drinks that start the process of getting drunk. The cycle repeats itself into the early morning hours. We are eventually kicked out of the pub to stagger around the streets of London.

Our wandering takes us across the path of another drunken airman. He stands outside a closed pub, belligerently yelling he wants his Half and Half *(beer).*

A man dressed in his nightgown appears in the second floor window. He opens it and dumps a bucket of piss on the head of the drunken airman's. He hollers to the sergeant below, "There's your Half and Half. Half mine, and half the old lady's."

Woo wee! That is funny. We laugh at the airman as he staggers away cursing a blue streak. We finally wander into a hotel and get a room to sleep off the night's adventure.

We stretch our stay in London as long as we can. We grudgingly hop on the train that takes us back. Everybody knows inside that they are returning to Old Buck to possibly die. Who wants to climb in a plane and die? I volunteered for this and duty calls. If my pals can get on the train, so can I.

We share stories of home to occupy our minds as we ride back. It doesn't work. I can see the image of that B-24 taking a direct hit plain as day. That guy that bailed out should have made it. The Krauts made sure he didn't. He was gunned down in his chute. He was no more than a legless torso floating out of the sky.

I can't shake the image of the guy floating by without a parachute. He didn't squirm or anything. He just fell, accepting his fate. I can still see blood and guts being hosed out of that tail turret just so a replacement could take that poor bastards place.

Once again, that weight bears down on me. I want to run and hide. I will not, this is my job. How can I let the guys down? Somewhere between the train station and Old Buck, we once again pick up our eleventh crew member. He is always on our heels. He looms over us, filling us with that dread feeling.

All the members of Crew 41 have made it back from a most perilous mission into London. As we go about preparing for the business of war, the base physician enters the barracks. The doc boldly announces, "Drop your pants and peel them back." We stand at attention with our pants down around our knees. Everybody checks out O.K, no social diseases here. We relive the highlights of our leave as we go about our duties.

March 14th; no flying for us today. I don't have to worry about getting killed, but other aircrews do. Not all the bombers in the group fly every mission but there are missions being flown almost daily. All the planes go up when there is a maximum effort.

We have "Lucky Penny" back. We go out and inspect her. The ground crew is already going over her with a fine toothed comb. It is their baby and she will not fail a mission because of a mistake on their part. Nick and Luther sit in the cockpit familiarizing themselves with the upgrades. Everybody inspects their improved bomber then returns to the barracks.

We do our housekeeping, chop wood and write letters to loved ones. A letter from my mom brings me infuriating news. She tells me my brother has enlisted. That dumb bastard. I would knock his head off if I was home. Who is going to watch mom and the girls?

The sound of returning bombers fills the air. I don't know if they are ours. It could be the bombers of any of the surrounding groups.

Suddenly the shrill sound of the air raid siren carries across the base. What the? We look to each other for...BOOM, BOOM, BOOM. Bombs, landing in the field next to the base! Is it the bomb dump? I don't think so. Maybe the fuel dump?

A mad dash is made for the trench behind the hut. Everybody dives headlong into the muddy slit. We slip and slide cursing as we fall over each other. BOOM, BOOM, more bombs. Huge clods of earth are tossed skyward. Shrapnel and debris whiz through the air. The concussion is tremendous. As quick as the raid starts, it is over. Nerves are tingling and ears ring. Holy crap, so that's what it is like to be on the receiving end of an attack.

The Kraut's missed their target. The bombs landed in

the adjacent field. Turwilliger starts giggling at the sight of everybody covered in mud. The crew finally breaks into uncontrollable laughter. Derogatory comments increase the humor of this dirty situation. We look like a bunch of pigs wallowing in the mud. We are a collective mess but we are an alive mess.

We later find out the Germans followed a flight of our bombers in. The Krauts pretended to be part of another bomb group. They stayed far enough behind so they would not attract any attention. From the ground, they looked like another bomber formation coming back. You have to give them dirty Krauts credit. It was a daring maneuver. The excitement of the day is washed away in the showers. Tomorrow it is back to the business of war, we will be playing with our lives again.

#7; Alerted; March 15th; Brunswick, Germany: Marshalling yards. We are awakened for the briefing at 2 A.M. We are told this will be a seven hour mission. After we grab our gear, the truck takes us out to Penny. It's good to have her back. She has carried us through our previous missions faithfully. We put our trust in this pile of aluminum and rivets that seems to take on a life of its own.

She has all the current upgrades. Nick nods in approval as he inspects his refurbished B-24 once again. He truly does appreciate the armor plates installed outside the cockpit. The plates are bolted under the cockpit glass on both sides of the plane. After everybody does a final walk around of Penny, we gear up for war.

Nick and Luther take their places in the cockpit. Luther announces, "Ignition switches on." Nick calls out. "Crack throttles," Luther replies, "Throttles cracked." Nick calls out, "Booster pumps," Luther replies, "Check." Prime engines, check. Starters energized, check. The two pilots rattle off the list. Luther sticks his hand out the window with three fingers in the air. "Clear on three," he shouts out. Moments later, the engine coughs to life. Soon Penny sits idling on her hardstand. The engines sound strong as they are run up, everything looks good.

"Lucky Penny" taxis out. Nick turns her onto the runway and we are off. We take our position on the edge of the circling formation. P-38s and P-47s escort us into Fortress Europe. I settle in for a long ride.

FLAK stains the clear blue sky as the strike force penetrates occupied territory. I hate this stuff. Come on Nick. Get us out of here. How long do I have to sweat it out this time? The formation mercifully breaks out of this angry, black cloud into a serene ocean of blue. This could mean only one thing, fighters.

Laddy reports Bandits, 6 o'clock low. There they are, I see them. Fw-190s, they are coming but still out of range. The Thunderbolts peel off into action. They drop like bricks on the Krauts.

It is brutal, the P-47s look like torpedoes with their noses cut off. The German pilots dive away in a frantic attempt to escape. Come on you fighter jocks. Get them Kraut bastards. The Jugs big radial engines chew up the sky as they power dive on their prey. The Huns do not have a chance in hell. The P47's close fast. The chase has to have taken them below 10,000 feet by now.

The first Focke Wolf attempts a climbing turn. This is a fatal mistake. The lead Thunderbolt hoses .50 caliber rounds into it. The Fw-190 starts to disintegrate. Pieces of plane tumble back in the slipstream. The port wing fragments. The fighter starts to barrel roll uncontrollably. The canopy slides back on this mortally wounded plane. The pilot is tossed into the sky by the centrifugal force. A parachute blossoms over his head. This German will live.

A second Fw-190 is finished as soon as it starts to pull out of its dive. The P-47 rakes the fuselage with its eight .50 caliber guns. The devastated German plane erupts into flames immediately. Another burst blows the canopy off the fire-engulfed cockpit. Flames spew the length of the fighter. The pilot remains strapped in his flaming coffin. This Focke Wolf blossoms into a huge crimson fireball as it cartwheels across the ground. The Thunderbolts execute victory rolls as they zoom climb back to altitude.

"Lucky Penny" lurches upward. I know the sensation. Leslie reports, "Bombs away." O.K. Nick, now let's get out of here. The formation begins the return leg home. It is a comforting feeling to have fighters with us. We are not harassed by FLAK on the way out. I constantly search the skies for enemy fighters that do not appear.

I can't stop shivering even with the midday sun shining in the turret. The cold chills the bones on these long hauls. I sit for hours on my little seat, looking into a blue void. It's lonely way up here so far away from home.

After what seems like forever, the cliffs of Dover come into sight. Once over East Anglia, the group transitions into a holding pattern above Station #144. The ritual begins. One by one, bombers turn on final approach and land.

Our pilot prepares to bring Penny in. The engines are set for full power at the push of the throttles. If there is a problem, we can power out of it. The flaps are set and the landing gear are lowered. Nick flares Penny out as we touch down.

Our B-24 rolls out to the end of the runway. Nick immediately turns Penny onto the taxi ramp. The strip must be cleared quickly so the remaining aircraft can land. Penny is brought to her hardstand and parked. After she is shut down, a tired crew emerges from her.

Before anybody can get their gear off, I pull the chord on Laddy's Mae West. The bottle of compressed air inflates the yellow life preserver with a hiss. We compliment Laddy on his beautiful rack as he jokingly struts around us. Luther can't stop laughing. There are giggles and snickers as we light up a couple of smokes.

Major Stewart yells out from his jeep, "How did it go Black Fury?" "Good, sir," I reply. Major Stewart gives me a nod. The officers gather in front of the plane, reviewing the mission. The truck arrives to take us to the debriefing. Once there, we idly standby waiting our turn.

After a shot of rum, the debriefing officers take a report from every crewman of every plane. Every man answers the interrogator's particular questions to the best of their ability. Each man's interview is like a piece of a mosaic. When all the pieces are put together, a picture of the raid comes into focus. This way the brass can get an accurate idea of what went on over a target.

After debriefing, we take a slow walk to the mess hall. I could use a cup of coffee. I do not feel well at all. I have no appetite, and my throat is raw. I can't shake this cough, I have to go lay down.

As soon as we enter the barracks, I go straight to my rack. I feel hot under my sheets. I know I'm sick, but I don't care. I have to stay with the crew. Besides, we have Penny back. She carried us home again. Our bomber now has seven bombs and two kills painted on her. I toss and turn through the night.

#8; Alerted; March 16th; Friedrichshafen, Germany: Aircraft factory. In briefing, we are told we will be hitting a factory about a half mile from the Swiss border. We take our customary ride to the plane. We are greeted by the usual English weather, damp, cold and cloudy.

After running down the checklist, our pilots bring Penny to life. Nick spurs her off the hardstand onto the ramp. The idling propellers carry us to the end of the runway where we sit.

The line of bombers wait for the signal to go. Moments later a green flare arcs into the pale light of a cloudy new day. The 453rd starts to take to the sky once again. Nick slowly brings Penny onto the runway. With a roar of the engines, we take flight. The Pratt & Whitney's bellow their full power song as we climb over the windmill that stands sentinel at the end of the strip.

Luther raises the flaps slowly as we gain airspeed. The cylinder head temperature looks good as we climb into the overcast. After anxious moments, Penny breaks out of the clouds at 10,000 feet. Luther turns the fuel pump boosters on. A vapor lock will kill an engine in an instant.

Contrails surround us as we take our position on the

edge of our assigned element. The 453rd links up with the other groups as we fly a humongous circuit over East Anglia. This is called Bunching. We fly these circuits until all the groups in the raid take their place. Once all the aircraft are assembled, the formation turns to Nazi, Germany. The journey to Friedrichshafen begins.

My throat and ears really hurt when I swallow. It's nothing a shot of oxygen can't cure. Once I settle into my turret, I get my Rosary out. I watch our Mustang escorts approach from the southwest. The P-51s fly criss-cross patterns above us as I pray.

The Mustangs carry drop tanks under each wing. It is hard to believe they are made out of paper. If it wasn't for the extra fuel they carry, there would be no such thing as fighter escort deep into enemy territory. Hours are spent peering into a vast blue sky as we take our indirect course to the target.

My rundown state doesn't help the situation. I feel like shit. It is miserable sitting here in the cold. My toes hurt, they tingle. The boredom is broken by fits of coughing. The only thing that breaks the monotony is the occasional joke. Some of them are really bad. I shake my head at how pathetic they are.

Leslie's voice breaks through loud and clear, "FLAK ahead." Like magic it appears. Angry black bursts fill the sky. All I can do is sit here and cringe. Penny crosses the threshold into the barrage. I have to be crazy to just sit here and wait to get killed. There is no alternative. I have to take it.

As soon as the formation clears the FLAK, a voice calls out, "Bandits." The fighter jocks spot them about the same time. The Mustangs drop their tanks and peel off. The melee is on. The P-51s dive out of the sun into the German formation. Moments later, two Krauts fall from the sky. They probably never saw it coming.

The first Fw-190 took hits from the cockpit forward. It suddenly pulled vertical. White puffs of coolant streamed from the engine as the propeller slowly ground to a halt. The fighter glided until it stalled. The plane then tumbled out of the sky. No doubt, the pilot is dead.

The second Kraut took hits across the wing and over the engine cowling. The Focke Wolf immediately started streaming black smoke. The pilot flipped the wounded bird on its back and ejected the canopy. The Kraut fell free from the inverted plane. He has guts. He made sure he fell clear of the dog fight before he opened his parachute.

The battle to get inside the other guys turn is on. Another Fw-190 falls victim to the Mustang. The pilot bails out. There is no mercy today. What you reap is what you sow. A P-51 lines up and let's loose with a quick burst. The bullets rip the defenseless pilot to pieces. A headless, half torso and leg float to the ground under a fluttering parachute. The fuckin bastards can have a taste of their own medicine.

A Focke Wolf hammers a P-51 with a nice deflection shot. The Kraut lands cannon rounds in the Mustang's belly. The P-51 takes the burst under the cockpit at the wing root. Fluid streams out of a radiator blown to pieces. Huge flames leap from the exhaust pipes. The wing folds up as the pilot flips his Mustang upside down.

A head and shoulders appear before the pilot falls free. This guy continues to fall, no parachute to be seen. He is a goner. Falling well out of range of the action, a parachute finally does open. I'm sure he didn't want to be another corpse under a canopy. If he can't reach the Swiss border, he will be a prisoner of war.

Another Mustang falls prey to the Butcher Bird. There appears to be nothing wrong as it starts to slow roll. The control surface linkages must be shot up or the pilot is dead. The Fw-190 trails the Mustang but does not need to fire another burst. The pristine Mustang begins to roll faster and faster. This plane is going to corkscrew itself right into the ground. The plane does a rolling power dive that ends in a violent explosion.

The Mustangs finally drive the Fw-190s off, but the Luftwaffe's plan works. The twin-engine Me-110s stay just out of the bombers machine gun range. They lob 20mm cannon rounds at us from a safe distance. There isn't any hope for me if a burst from a Me-110 finds its mark. It will blow me and the turret apart.

Sinister orange balls spit from under the Me-110's nose as the pilot fires his cannons at me. The rounds grow larger as they approach. They appear as glowing orange beach balls. The Hun shoots just wide of Penny.

It is a frightening sight. With some Kentucky Windage, I pop off a few short bursts at the Kraut bastard. I have to disrupt this pilot's aim before I get killed. My tracers arc out across the sky. The Me-110 dips a wing then levels off again. My shots must be close enough to unnerve him.

The Me-110 unleashes another burst. The tracers grow larger then pass under Penny. Finally, the Mustangs return and drive those god damn Me-110s off. They dive away out of sight.

Penny lurches up with the familiar call of "Bombs away." The formation immediately turns for home. It is a long way back. Crew 41 stares intently into the blue sky as we wait for another attack. Nick reports, "FLAK ahead." Once again, I crouch on my seat. All I can do is sweat it out. CRUMPH, Nick starts his dance across the sky again.

As I watch a B-24 in our box take a hit, anger and fear erupt inside. I silently root for the crew. Come on guys, get out. The number two engine has been blown off its mount. It tumbles away with the propeller spinning.

The pilot's side of the cockpit glass is shattered. The bomber starts its violent trip to earth. The Liberator flat spins out of the sky. A crazy corkscrew of smoke traces the path to its demise. The centrifugal force pins those guys where they are. They are riding it all the way in. That is no way to go.

The formation breaks free of the barrage into the clear. It looks like we lost some planes, better them than me. Death is so random. The escorts shepherd the crippled bombers as they limp home. The ambulances and crash trucks will be waiting for them when we return.

YEEOUCH, that stings! My face is on fire as I take my oxygen mask off. It really hurts. My chin and cheeks are burning. Oh no, I know what happened. I tore the skin off of my face. The moisture of my breath froze the mask to my skin. When I adjusted it, I didn't feel it tear my face in the 40 below temperature.

The formation finally returns home. Penny starts flying circuits over Old Buck. I go into fits of coughing as we wait to land. With a squeal of the tires, we touch the runway ten minutes later. The bomb bay doors are opened as we taxi to the hardstand.

After Penny is shut down, a tired crew gets out of their flight gear. Nick walks over to check me out. He tells me, "Your face looks bad; you better go to the infirmary." I shake my head in agreement. I do not feel good at all. I sit sweating under Penny's wing. The cigarette burns the back of my throat as we wait for the truck.

At interrogation, I am again urged to go see the doctor. After I am debriefed, I go to the base hospital. The flight surgeon examines me and dresses my wound. My face will be bandaged for a while. I am told, I am also on the verge of pneumonia. The doctor informs me that I am grounded. I protest, "I can't be, I will lose my crew." "Sorry, sergeant," the doctor reiterates, "You are grounded."

The news is upsetting. I don't want to miss a mission. I want to finish with the guys. What can I do? Disgusted, I accept my fate. Oh well, I do feel pretty raw and my face burns. I will take my medicine like a man and hit the rack. There are three days until we fly again. I have to get well enough to get back in that bomber.

The next day, I feel good enough to go into town with Laddy. We decide to go see a movie. We happen across Nick with a date in the theater. He does not know we are there so we sneak up behind him.

Nick is the boss but we can't help ourselves. We crouch behind him as he sits with his arm around his date. I reach up and pet Nick's hand. He cuddles his date closer. I do this a few more times and get the same results. Laddy and I can hardly keep from laughing out loud. I motion to Laddy, "Let's get out of here." We sneak out of the theater and leave Nick to his own devices.

Of course, we run into Nick later. His date is still with him. He tells us more than asks us if we are staying out of trouble. He is no worse for the wear. Maybe we did him a favor. He has no clue we were in the theater. Laddy and I have a drink at the local pub before we return to Old Buck. I will know soon enough if I will be able to fly.

#9; Alerted; March 18th; Friedrichshafen, Germany: We will be going there again. We are to expect FLAK and fighters. I am not going though. I am grounded, but I still go out to the plane with the guys. I tell them, "See you later." I hope I do, as I watch them climb aboard. Nick fires our bomber up and rolls off the hardstand. Penny taxis down the ramp to the end of the airfield with the other bombers. Penny swings on the runway and she is gone.

The group disappears into the distance. What a lonely feeling. I should be with them, damn it. What if they do not come back? What if there was something I could have done? If they die, I should die with them. What if the guy in the tail doesn't see the Kraut fighters until it is too late? I hope he is good. He is protecting my buddies. Damn, I should be there. Damn this pneumonia and screw the frostbite.

Now I know how the ground personnel feel. I linger with them at the hardstand. We talk about anything to keep the bombers off our minds. Some guys go into ritualistic routines in an attempt to keep busy.

Some of the ground crews play catch. I wonder how the Yankees will be this year. Others toss a football around. I do not ask to join in with any of them. I do not want to interfere with any of their superstitious rituals. I play with the tools in the shed instead.

We go to the ground crew mess hall for lunch. There isn't any carrying on with us, everything is kind of subdued. In other areas of the mess hall, there is laughter and loud conversation.

It is easy to tell which ground crews have a plane flying

today, just by the mood at the tables. No matter, they all get their turn sweating it out for their plane. After lunch, we hop on our bikes and pedal back out to the hardstand.

Leaning against a 55-gallon drum, I contemplate the idea of Penny not coming back. I begin to wonder which ground crews will not have a plane to work on in a few hours. These guys like issuing light-hearted warnings to the aircrews. "Don't lose my plane," is a common refrain. They are just masking their fear with false audacity.

They know they may be talking to the aircrew for the last time when they prepare the plane. They do not control the FLAK or fighters, but questions gnaw at the back of their minds. They wonder as they wait for their plane to return. Was it prepared well? Is the plane doomed because of something overlooked? Lives are literally riding in the bombers these guys prepare.

The ground crew asks me about combat. I reply," What do want to know?" I tell them what it's like to watch a bomber get shot down. I describe the helpless feeling of being caught in a FLAK barrage.

They shake their heads as they imagine what I describe. They picture the raid on Berlin. They enjoy the story of our single-handed attack on the train depot in France. The guys grunt in disbelief or agreement as I describe a particular incident.

Restlessness sets in as the hours pass. Some ground crews stay at their hardstands. Some are at their barracks sleeping. These guys were up all hours repairing their respective planes. Some were wrangling with chronic problems through the night, just to have their plane ready for today. The mission weighs heavy on their minds also. They fear they may be the cause of an empty hardstand.

The crash trucks and the fire crews wait. A crippled bomber could appear at any given moment. The guys in the silver fire suits with the little glass window to see out of, they are brave. They wade right into a high octane fire to get a guy. The crash crews chop wrecked planes apart to save lives. They are definitely our unsung heroes.

The ambulance crews deal with human misery. These

guys are angels of mercy to a wounded or dying airman. They dedicate their lives so an airman may live. They are there before a B-24 stops sliding down the runway. They are there to gently pick a wounded airman off of the fuselage floor. They remove the lifeless body in the pilot's seat or turret. They retrieve the human remains from a twisted wreck that was once a bomber. These brave men look human suffering in the face time after time.

Word is past down from the control tower. The bombers are on their way. The waiting officers gather at the control tower. All eyes look skyward in the general direction of the approaching planes. The crash crews are ready. The ambulance crews wait by their trucks.

Little specks that are the bombers appear in the distance. Everybody counts them as they approach. Did "Lucky Penny" make it? The planes are too far away to tell.

Ten of the sixteen start to circle overhead. Is Penny with them? More specks, only five. We are one short. Is it Penny? The bombers begin circling the base in a holding pattern. There aren't any red flares. Good, no wounded crew or crippled planes. The 453rd starts to come in. A Liberator lands after every circuit. Maybe this last plane will come later.

We wait in anticipation for Penny at the hardstand. A smile cracks across my worried face as she comes into view. The Pratt & Whitneys sound like some angry animals as the bomber taxis down the ramp. The high performance engines snort and pop as Nick parks our Liberator. Boy, does that sound good. After Penny is directed into place, Nick shuts her down.

The guys slowly emerge from under the plane. I am elated to see them. I need every detail of the mission. Turwilliger tagged an Me-109. No doubt about it. It dove away and exploded. "Lucky Penny" had a good day.

It was not the case for everybody. Nick tells me Col. Miller was shot down. That's too bad; all I know is my crew is safe. I don't have to think, what if, the rest of my life.

We find out in debriefing that Col. Miller was indeed shot down, just over the Swiss border. He was the groups commanding officer. I don't know if the crew made it or not. I do know the show must go on. We will get a new group commander regardless. After a late dinner, we retire to the hut. I hit my rack just happy the guys made it.

It's something how the ground crew has to put up with a mission. They sweat it out on the ground. They walk around with a dark cloud over their heads all day. Those guys are alright.

After I put an entry in my diary, I say my prayers. We have two days until we fly again. I am now one mission behind the guys. I hope the doctor gives me the O.K. to fly.

#10; Alerted; March 23rd; Munster, Germany: We are awakened at 1:45 A.M. I was given the O.K. to fly yesterday. It is only right to be with the guys again.

In briefing, we are told Munster will be punished. We are asserting our dominance once more. We will pound another city, of Hitler's Germany, into submission. The planes will be armed with general-purpose bombs, incendiaries and napalm. I don't like this.

After we get our parachutes, we gather at the truck. We throw our gear on, and ride out to the plane. As soon as we reach the hardstand, I peer into Penny's belly. Incendiaries, I really hate them. I imagine Penny going up like the biggest Roman Candle that ever existed from even a minor hit. I don't like this at all.

Nick and Luther go through the preflight checklist as we prepare for the mission under Penny's wing. When everybody is ready, Nick fires the bomber up. I wait as usual until each engine is brought to an idle. All is good. I quickly pass the incendiaries as I climb aboard.

Penny's landing lights lead the way as we taxi down the ramp. Nick brings our bomber onto the runway. With a push of the throttles, we climb into the predawn sky. The formation climbs over the channel in the faint light of a new day. This day will bring destruction to Munster.

I strap on my oxygen mask as we climb to our cruising

altitude. Hah, a guy sitting in a turret at 25,000 feet over Fortress Europe is called the Western Front. There aren't any troops on the ground, but the Army Air Corps has been conducting huge raids. We hit the Krauts where it hurts. We destroy aircraft production, transportation and oil. We wage our war with Germany from the sky. One day, we will put troops on the ground.

As they fight us, the Nazis fight pitched battles with the Russians on the Eastern Front. The winter weather has really hurt them. It's starting to look like a lost cause. The Luftwaffe has begun transferring fighter squadrons to the West in defense of the Father Land.

CRUMPH, CRUMPH, Nick calls out," FLAK ahead." The brackets of anti-aircraft start coming up. CRUMPH, CRUMPH, this stuff is wicked. I wince in my turret. The Kraut gunners are locked in on our course and altitude this time. They have us bracketed.

The FLAK is heavy, so heavy. I wish I was on the ground sick again. Why do I want to be here and die? Why did I feel guilty waiting for the guys to come back? I'm trapped in this plexiglas cage with nowhere to hide.

BANG, shrapnel peppers the bomber. It sounds like gravel is being thrown at the plane. Penny jerks slightly from a near miss. It was Nick's instinctive reaction to a burst going off near the cockpit. He jerked the yoke as he intuitively ducked for cover. Not a thing can be done about it, we are helpless. Nick's little bracket game is all we got. It does work, so far.

My legs are weak and I swallow hard. I pray for salvation inside this dark cloud of doom. It scares me to death every time. A guy would have to be crazy to get used to this. I pray to God, let me make it. Let...BANG, more holes are punched into Penny by another near miss.

Laddy reports the ball turret is jammed. It will not move or retract. He cannot get out. Victor informs Nick that there isn't any visible damage he can see. Nick tells Victor and Turwilliger to get him out.

Turwilliger grabs an axe while Victor grabs a crowbar. A good whack and some prying rotates the turret so the hatch can be opened. The door flips up and Laddy scrambles out. He will ride in the waist through the rest of this FLAK ridden hell.

The punishment of Munster is visible from miles away. It is wracked with bombs. The column of smoke rising from the city beckons the bombers to it like moths. Penny lurches as we unload our incendiaries on the target. We add fuel to a burning city. Munster is being gutted.

Damn this FLAK, it will not quit. I should strap on my parachute and bail out. This is madness, the anti-aircraft just keeps coming.

Evasive action scatters bombers across the sky. Nick calls out," Does anybody see our group?" We know they are out there, but we are praying just to make it out of this alive. Finally, we emerge from the angry, black cloud. Where's the group, let alone our element? Not a B-24 to be seen. We have lost our group.

A loner out here is certain doom. We got away with it once. Once is one time too many. Leslie spots a B-17 group in the distance. We tune to their frequency and report we will be joining up with them. Nick throttles back as we fall in on the lower edge of their formation.

P-47s and P-38s fly along with us. I cannot believe it; those B-17 guys always have it made. We are not harassed the rest of the way home. We peel off over Norfolk.

There's the windmill. We don't need to get in a landing pattern because the sky is empty. The group is coming home piecemeal. Nick brings Penny straight in. We quickly turn off the runway onto the taxi ramp. Penny's idling engines pull us to our hardstand. After the brakes are applied, Nick shuts her down.

I truly appreciate the smiling faces of the ground crew. Those guys are great. A smoke really tastes good after this mission. It was a rough one. We climb on the waiting truck that carries us to interrogation.

The shot of brandy goes down easy as I take my turn debriefing. After I am finished, I step aside so the other guys can be interviewed. I'll wait for them to finish so we can go to the mess hall together. The meal tastes better than ever today. What a day. We got shot up pretty good, but the rat bastard Krauts didn't get us.

When I get to the shack, I put an entry in my diary. I say my prayers and lay down. It has been a harrowing day and I am dead tired. We have two days off until we fly again. I'll wait until tomorrow to take a shower.

The next day, Laddy, Joe and I take a leisurely walk down the road to the local pub for dinner. Fish and Chips are what we have. Fish and Chips are what the English live on. Fish and Chips are all there is. It is greasy as all hell, but it is good. So, we enjoy a meal of Fish and Chips with a few beers.

The British kids always stand outside the pub looking in the windows. They just watch people eat. They are poor; the war has done this to many families. When we finish our dinner, I look at them trying to get their attention. When I do, I put my finger upward in a wait gesture.

We buy extra Fish and Chips before leaving. We hand the kids the greasy, paper bags full of food. We get the biggest smiles from these youngsters. They run away screaming and laughing. They yell out, "Thanks, Yanks," as they hurry home. A few families will have a treat tonight.

#11; Alerted; March 26th; Domart, France: Coastal batteries. We will not be going deep into enemy territory for this mission. It makes no difference; you can get shot down anywhere. We are told to expect FLAK and fighters. We are shown the route we will take and our assigned altitudes. We will have P-38s escorting us. We walk out of the briefing into the mud.

It is a mushy, muddy mess everywhere. There are pallets and planks to walk on, but your feet are eventually covered with the slop. If you step off the boards, you're dirty. I hate that. I hate having mud in the plane. The other guys change into their flight boots at the hardstand, but I always have to give my shoes a good cleaning.

The topic of discussion as we gear up for the mission is the weather. The conversation turns to home and family. It inevitably leads to the dreaded FLAK. Nick yells, "Let's go," from the cockpit window. We boost Powell in the plane with the customary, "Come on, Tiger."

After all the engines are running, I duck under the plane into the bomb bay. I hop on the catwalk and glance at the fuel transfer lines on the bulkhead. Everything looks good.

The crew waits in takeoff positions. Laddy, Victor and Turwilliger are standby near the ball turret well. Leslie, Powell and I are with Joe Craft. Nobody goes into the nose until we are airborne. If the nose gear collapses or we crash, that is a bad place to be.

Hansen is on the flight deck with the pilots. The main reason the crew takes these positions is to get everybody as close as possible to the plane's center of gravity. This makes Penny easier to fly during takeoff.

Nick closes the bomb bay doors before we roll off the hardstand. Hansen sits in the opened escape hatch behind the cockpit. He helps Nick with forward vision as we taxi down the ramp. He will button Penny up before we takeoff. Our plane joins the procession of bombers moving down the line. The big radial engines idle as we patiently wait our turn to take to the sky.

When it's time to go, Nick swings Penny onto the runway and we're off to war again. Luther synchronizes the propellers as we climb to join the circling bombers. Nick slides Penny into her usual position on the edge of our assigned element.

The formation turns for France. Domart awaits its fate. Our flight path takes us over Abbeville. No Yellow Nosed Bastards to greet us, but the Germans begin to fill the sky with anti-aircraft. The FLAK dogs us as we push on to the target. CRUMPH, CRUMPH, Nick slides in and out of the brackets. Carter joins us in our dance across the sky.

Damn, it's cold. What the hell! No wonder I'm freezing, my heated suit is not working. Yes, it is plugged in. What a piece of shit. There is most likely a short in it.

There are a limited number of these heated suits in service. They are trucked back and forth from base to base. The British use them at night and we use them during the day. Well, mine is not working. What else is new? No point reporting it to Nick. I can't do anything about it. Ehh, it isn't so bad. I just want to get another mission under my belt, one more step closer to home.

Searching the sky is second nature by now. No FLAK or fighters to be seen. We turn on the Initial Point. We fly straight and level at the assigned altitude. Leslie reports, "Bombs away." Penny lurches up as the bombs fall free.

The target comes into view as the formation passes over it. From my Skybox seat, I watch the bombs saturate the gun emplacements. It looks like a good strike. A column of smoke rises from the target area.

Light FLAK harasses us as the formation turns for home. Be it light or not, I don't like it. It only takes one well placed round to kill me. We fly over Amiens, no fighters here either. We cross the channel unmolested. Instead of being terrorized, I am just cold and scared today.

The channel looks frigid. I wouldn't want to ditch. The B-24 floats like a rock. You have to get out and into a raft quickly. If you stay in the water too long, hypothermia will get you.

If there is a buoy nearby, you could swim or paddle over to it. Once inside you are relatively safe. The British keep them stocked with food, water and blankets. You still have to be vigilant. The Krauts and British patrol the channel; they race to recover any downed airmen. Nobody wants to fall into the hands of the enemy.

Trains move supplies up and down coastal routes as we cross into England. The 453rd flies into Norfolk and takes up a racetrack pattern until all the planes come in.

The mission wasn't too bad. I follow Nick and Luther around the plane as they count the FLAK hits. The tally is two, not bad. Penny has been patched up quite a bit, but she is a good girl. She carries us home time after time.

I never noticed how many silver B-24s are here now.

Staff Sergeant Edmund Survilla.

Crew 41, Top - Burgess, Hubbard, Radosevich, Miller, Head. Bottom - Turwilliger, Hansen, Craft, Survilla, Victor.

B-24 tail turret.

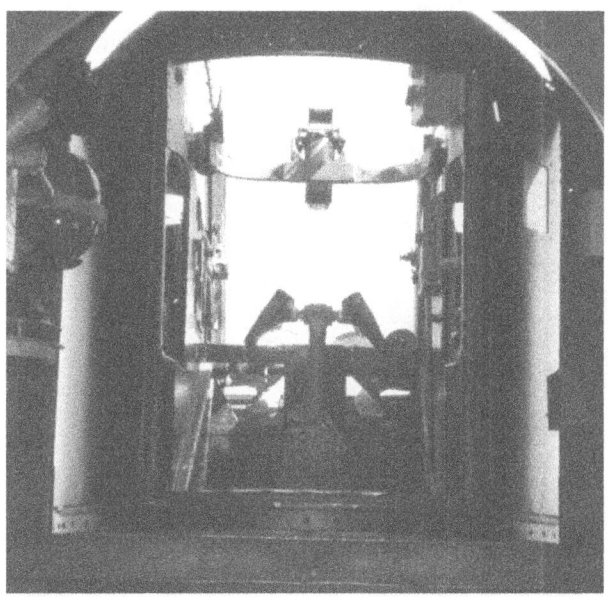

Inside a B-24 tail turret, the control stick and gun sight are clearly visible.

Crew 41, in flight at March Field. The "Reluctant Dragon" flies on their wing.

Crew 41, in flight at March Field. Hansen takes another photo of a B-24 practicing formation flying.

A look into the locked cockpit of a B-24. The photograph is taken from the radioman's compartment.

The ground crew of "Lucky Penny" stand next to their new Liberator. There will not be a failure on their part.

A B-24 taxis out. The flight engineer stands in the escape hatch. This was done to aid the pilot with forward vision.

Crew 41 and ground crew with their new B-24. *(It is before the 19th mission.)* Standing - ground crew, Survilla, Lee, Clark, ground crew, ground crew, Turwilliger, ground crew, ground crew. Kneeling - ground crew, ground crew, Head, Hansen, Powell. Sitting - ground crew Craft, Victor. Laying- Radosevich. The Roman numeral two is outlined in chalk after "Lucky Penny." It has yet to be painted in.

Crew 41, *(This photo was taken the same time as previous photo.)* Back - Survilla, Lee, Radosevich, Clark, Turwilliger. Front - Head, Hansen, Craft, Victor. Powell is behind the camera. *(Bandage can be seen on Edmund's chin.)*

In the mess hall. Back - Laddy Head, Rob Hansen. Front - Charlie *(the cook)*, Edmund Survilla.

Crash landed B-24 at R.A.F. base.

D-Day debriefing at the plane. From the left - Intelligence officer, Victor, Craft, Powell, Radosevich, Hansen, Clark. intelligence officer, ground crew, ground crew. The new tail markings are visible.

Crew 41, just after completing final mission. From the left - Powell, Radosevich, Survilla, Lee, Craft, Victor, Head. Standing with back to camera - Turwilliger, Hansen, Clark. *(U.S.A.A.C. # 81891AC. Photo by, Albert de laGarza.)*

Edmund *(Black Fury)* Survilla, 2003.

Did we lose that many of the original cadre? There is more bare aluminum Liberators here than I thought. They are the J models. Yes, aircraft do get used up and are declared war-weary, but you still have the original crew. These guys get shiny new birds.

I do not fool myself; there are a lot of guys that are dying. There are many new faces and they look eager for the fight. They are idiots, they don't know what they are getting into.

Pssssssttttt, they got me! My Mae West inflates. I quickly turn around and look at the guys with a grin. I put one hand on my head and one on my hip. I strike a pose and tell the guys the tale of the girl I laid on our last leave. Laughter is the reply I get. The guys throttle me as we undress.

We enjoy a smoke as the truck takes us to debriefing. We stand in line and wait to be interrogated. I harass Laddy as the line slowly moves forward. We carry on as the crewmembers in front of us are interviewed.

When I am debriefed, I answer the questions I am asked. The officer scribbles the relevant information down, then jokingly tells me to get lost. Laddy takes his turn next.

When the guys are finished, we go to the mess hall for a bite. Nobody pays attention to anybody else. Nobody wants the face of another dead man to remember. After we chow down, we head to our barracks. I want to get cleaned up and lay down. It would be nice to hear from home. I hope I got some mail.

#12; Alerted; March 27th; Pau, France: Luftwaffe training base. This will be a long one, over ten hours. No getting around it. We truck out to Penny and suit up for the mission. POW, POW, POW, POW. Startled faces turn in the direction of the unmistakable sound of a .50 caliber machine gun.

Everybody looks down the line to the next set of hardstands. A Liberator sits awkwardly on its pad. It leans over like some giant, crippled bird. The waist gunner just shot up the landing gear. He practically blew the tire off the rim. Of course, it was an accident. "I don't know what happened," is the answer.

No mission for that crew. I know people get cold feet. I know fear will drive people to do funny things, but it's not right. I call it chicken shit. Everybody else is putting their lives on the line. We have a final cigarette before we climb aboard. It is time to go; we have to stay on schedule. We will take our chances again.

Penny is fired up and we're off into a dim, gray sky. Our plane climbs to join the circling formation. We fall in on the edge of the group. We continue to circle as the rest of the bombers form up. We turn for Europe.

I study the bomber behind us with interest. The pilots methodically search the skies. The bombardier climbs into the nose turret. He quickly scans his surroundings. The turret swings back and forth as he makes sure everything is working properly. He points the guns forward and searches the horizon.

Here we go again, hours of being cold and doing nothing. I must stay vigilant. The moment that my mind drifts could be the end for me or the crew. There isn't any sign of the enemy as I adjust my mask.

It is cold but the drone of the engines is comforting. The sun shining on my face is warm. It feels good; it helps battle the cold that slowly saps the energy out of me. My eyes begin to strain from searching the skies for hours.

CRUMPH, I cower on my seat again. Penny enters a barrage of FLAK. Moments later, we exit it untouched. It should always be like that.

These missions are stretching me to the limit. A person is not supposed to function under these stresses on a regular basis. The hours drag on. My mind wants to drift. I think of my dad. I think of Siracourt and almost getting killed. I fight the urge to doze off.

As we approach the target, the dreaded FLAK starts again. A black curtain of anti-aircraft descends upon us. CRUMPH, CRUMPH, Nick announces the lead bomber is going down. I only see the remnants of a huge, flaming ball of fire. The black smoke trail traces the path back to where the FLAK shell hit home.

Everybody looking forward saw the spectacle. The lead plane took a direct hit, just forward of the bomb bay. An explosion erupted from between the wings. An instant later, they tore away from the plane. The fuselage blew in half forward of the bomb bay. The bombs tumbled crazily out of the fireball only to impact on some indiscriminant location.

The cockpit forward continued leading the way until its momentum died out. It then began to barrel roll as it arced downward. After the fuel burned off, the remnants of the violent encounter tumbled from the sky.

All I see is a black trail of smoke with men and parts falling away. They just fall away. Some of the limp bodies tumble as they fall out of sight. In a moment, the sky will wipe the fierce encounter away like it never happened.

I shudder at the thought of taking that long ride to the ground. To be trapped in a plane, conscious all the way in, is no way to go.

The deputy lead bomber takes over. The marker bomb falls free. The formation follows the new leaders signal.

Gravity pulls general-purpose bombs earthward. They fall until they are no longer visible. The airfield erupts in an instant as salvos of bombs walk the length of the airstrip. The group repeatedly sweeps the runway under. The strike looks good. The formation wheels for the five hour ride home.

I hate this, hours of boredom and moments of terror. There is nowhere to hide when the action starts. You can face an enemy fighter down with your guns, but you're still not hiding from him. FLAK, there is nothing a person can do. You cannot save yourself. Your life is in the hands of another person that wants to kill you. Your fate rests upon his aim. It is simple as that.

Penny carries us home again. We fly a holding pattern over the base. Turwilliger excitedly yells out, "Take a look at the runway." In animated tones, he tells us to watch the planes coming in on final approach. A B-24 trails another way too close.

The lead bomber lands with the trailing B-24 riding up its tail. The first plane guns the throttles in a frantic attempt to escape destruction. The maneuver works. The lead bomber powers out of the situation with a touch and go.

The trailing bomber rolls to the end of the runway and quickly taxis clear of the strip. What an asshole! The dumb bastard of a pilot almost killed 20 guys. I hope he catches hell. He should have his dumb ass grounded.

After the near miss, Nick brings Penny in to her hardstand. What wonderful machines these are, that fly such great distances, five miles above the earth. Machines we are not. Exhausted, we emerge from under Penny. Tired limbs are stretched after a ten hour mission.

We debrief then get something to eat. I wolf down my food as we talk about the B-24 that took the direct hit. That was an olive drab bomber. That was one of the original planes. After two helpings of dinner, we wander off to our shack and relax. That was a long mission. I wonder how much of the original cadre we lost already. What day is it?

We thankfully have two weeks down time. We look sickly; nobody gets enough sleep. Nobody is eating right. Nerves are frayed and tensions run high. We deal with 40 below temperatures for hours.

The thought of dropping bombs on people does cross my mind. I wonder how many thousands of people the 453rd has killed already. How many people did "Lucky Penny" kill? So be it, I wouldn't be here if Nazi Germany didn't make war. The biggest stress that hangs over us is the specter of death. This is a dirty, stinking business. We'll make up for it in London.

It is time to live it up for a while. As soon as we arrive at Piccadilly Circus, Laddy, Leslie, Joe and I go get a drink. Girls join us at the table as we booze the night away. I wake up to find myself laying next to a girl in some flat. How I wound up here is beyond me. My host is a pretty girl with beautiful long brown hair. She has a nice rack too.

The attraction is mutual and the sex is great. The leave in London turns into an alcohol fueled relationship that is driven by sex. Who knows if I will be alive tomorrow, I live for today.

This hard playing isn't relaxation either. After a few days, I am content with the companionship of my new girlfriend. I spend the remainder of my leave shacking up with her.

When a guy really wants to convalesce, he can go to the 453rd's retreat. It is the chalet of a wealthy family. They have graciously opened their doors to the aircrews. It is a striking home with beautiful hardwood and high ceilings. The estate grounds are meticulously kept, it is beautiful. The family treats the aircrews like one of their own. It is fine living. What wonderful people they are.

A guy could also stay with an English family on his leave. It is as close to home as some of these guys will get before they die.

A guy could always play sports. There is constantly a football or baseball game being played on the base. Just being away from the bombers works wonders.

Powell is always out somewhere with his camera. Nick and Luther run with the other pilots. Leslie comes with us sometimes but he is usually with the officers.

Hansen and Turwillger are more family orientated. They like sightseeing and mingling with the locals. Victor is always somewhere doing something. Nobody knows where he goes. A leave always starts with hard drinking but ends up with thinking of home.

When the crew returns to Old Buck, everybody looks a hell of a lot better than they did two weeks ago. With everybody refreshed, we are ready to fly again.

The last of the guys sneaks into the hut just after everybody hits the rack. I notice purple around his neck. When he undresses, he is purple from his neck down. "What in the hell happened to you?" I ask. The mumbled reply I get is, "Crabs." "Crabs?", I say. Everybody in the hut replies, "Crabs?" "Ewwuu, yuck." We start laying into him. He is painted from the neck down with a purple medicine.

Someone yells, "You look like a fuckin pickled egg." He is ribbed mercilessly. Each comment brings more laughter. After we tire of brutally tormenting the dumb ass, we drift off to sleep amid sporadic giggles.

#13; Alerted; April 8th; Brunswick, Germany: Marshalling yards. We are told we will strike rail yards. The objective is to paralyze the Krauts, destroy their means of transportation and the goods they carry. We are told to expect FLAK and fighters. We will rendezvous with Thunderbolts. They will take us to the target and back.

We go to the parachute hangar and grab our chutes. I always wonder if I have picked a good one, this one better open. I've heard stories of damp parachutes freezing like bricks. I've seen guys fall to their death. We hop on the truck and ride out to the plane.

The preflight rituals begin. Layers of clothing are put on under the mechanic's jump suits. We put on our harnesses and Mae Wests. We grab our parachute bags and toss them in the plane. Nick yells out, "Let's go." I standby outside and watch the engines crank to life. Everything looks good.

We taxi out to join the line of bombers waiting to take flight. Our B-24 slowly moves down the ramp until we reach the head of the runway. Nick swings our bomber onto the strip in a continuous motion. The engines spring to life, Penny carries us to war.

The pins are pulled on the bombs before I go to my turret. I mentally prepare for the mission. Once again, I assume I am already dead. The turret is unlocked and I put on my mask. The guns are charged; I am ready to go. I search for our escorts through the gun sight. They do not show up. We are on our own.

The formation enters enemy territory under a crisp blue sky. Hmmm, marshalling yards, I wonder what kind of action we will see. Black specks come into view on the horizon. There they are out in the distance, fighters. I call out, "Bandits, 3 o'clock." A dogfight has erupted in the distance. The Krauts attack in two separate groups. They use one of these groups to tangle with the Thunderbolts. The other gaggle prepares to attack us.

Once again, they fly parallel to the formation until they are out ahead of us. The Krauts turn into the bombers head on. They attack line abreast. Leslie reports fifteen plus bandits dead ahead. The closing speed is amazing. In one pass, five bombers start to go down.

One of the bombers lurch upward as cannon fire blows the cockpit apart. Glass, metal and a red mist explode out of what was a working flight deck. It all washes away in the slipstream. What were two men at the controls, just moments ago, is no more. No doubt the top turret gunner and radio operator are dead too.

The plane abruptly pulls into a vertical climb until it stalls. It nearly flips on its back. The B-24 hangs in the sky for agonizing moments before it does a tail slip. The surrounding B-24s steer clear of this bomber. It finally does flip on its back. It falls upside down through the formation. A Liberator is not built to take such stresses and it begins to tear its self apart. Guys start to bail out as it falls away. They have to get out now.

A Liberator in our combat box has taken cannon rounds in the wing root. The hits send pieces of aluminum flying. The well-placed rounds tear this B-24 apart. Wow! The wing folds straight up and breaks off. This bomber instantly rolls over on its side, the good wing points straight up into the heavens. This plane begins to tumble crazily as it falls away.

Evasive action keeps the B-24s of the lower element from being struck by the dying Liberator and its wing. The stricken bomber passes through the formation and begins its final ride to earth. Nobody is getting out of that plane. It happened too quickly.

Yet another dips a wing and starts to dive. The remnants of two more Liberators tumble away in the distance. The sun dances across their aluminum bodies.

The Kraut bastards make another pass. As they slash

through the formation, I wait for my chance. I want another kill. A Me-109 shows its belly to Leslie. His guns bark and a few rounds find their mark. At the same time, Hansen hoses rounds into the belly of the Tin Can.

It's done. The mortally wounded fighter barrel rolls and dives away with pieces streaming behind it. The pilot is dead. Moments later, it explodes. It reminds me of a deranged firework. Hansen calls out, "Someone confirm that for me," Luther interjects, "Leslie got a piece of it, too." Turwilliger replies, "You're good."

We battle through the fighters only to fly into a wall of FLAK. We execute the raid in the midst of a vicious barrage. I hate this the most. We have to stay straight and level for the sake of the bomb run. No evasive action can be taken. The FLAK hammers away as we approach the release point. Leslie announces, "Bombs away." We turn for home. We come out of the barrage only to face head on attacks again.

The Jerries attack line abreast again. Those dirty bastards are usually diving away before I get my chance at them. Laddy shouts out," I got one! I got one!" I reply, "Way to go Laddy." Victor replies, "I saw it, I will confirm." The gun camera in his turret will confirm the kill also. As quick as the fighters appear, they are gone. I search a suddenly empty sky.

The formation loosens up for the return leg. Intercom checks break the monotony of the long journey. Hansen calls out, "Fighters at 2 o' clock." We wait for them to come close enough to make positive identification.

You can't miss that twin boom; they are P-38s. Thank God for the Lightnings. Where the hell are some of those Mustangs that can go anywhere we can? It would have been nice to have them with us. The Lightnings take us to the English coast before they peel off.

We have a few crippled bombers in the formation. They will land first. I don't know who is dead or dying in these planes. They fire red flares to signal they are in trouble. The crash trucks are ready. The ambulance crews standby. We fly circuits in the blue skies over Norfolk until all the battle damaged planes have landed. Twenty minutes later, Nick brings Penny in.

That was a hairy mission. We didn't do very well. Maj. Stewart drives up to us and yells out, "How did it go Black Fury?" I reply, "Sir, why do you call me Black Fury?" He tells me, "My jet-black hair reminds him of the horse in the movie, Fury." He gives me a smile and a wink. The officers climb in Maj. Stewart's jeep and drive off. The rest of us hop on the truck that takes us to debriefing.

After we are interrogated, we go to the mess hall. It's been a long day and I am hungry. Charlie the cook always has something special for us. After a hot meal, we settle down for the night.

Word is we lost seven planes today. I get out my map and trace the path of this mission. I enter this raid in my diary before I hit the sack. I drift off praying for the safety of the crew.

#14; Altered; April 9th; Tutow, Germany: Airfield. We will attack an airfield on Easter Sunday. We are to expect FLAK and fighters. This will be another long one. Our escorts will be Mustangs. We grab our chutes and ride out to the hardstand. We toss our gear off the truck in preparation of another attack.

I stand under Penny's wing as she is brought to life. She joins the other bombers as the 453rd taxis out. Nick swings Penny onto the runway and she carries us into the early morning sky.

I know every vibration, rattle and sound of "Lucky Penny." I know my station like the back of my hand. Our lives depend on it. I know how every paint chip and scratch got on the gear in my turret. I know the sound and feel of the equipment I am surrounded by. I know the quirks of my apparatus. Our Liberator is alive, and has a personality of Its own.

The formation climbs into the rarified air. Nick orders, "Oxygen masks on." I hook up and plug in. Sometimes one can't help but admire the beauty way up here. The formation flies stacked in combat boxes as we cruise to the target. The bombers pull contrails momentarily as we go through a temperature layer.

We enter Fortress Europe. The Krauts have adopted the policy of moving their fighters closer to Germany. The deeper we penetrate into Europe, the more the German high command moves its airbases back.

I think it is stupid. The Krauts are conceding ground gained at the outbreak of the war. One would think that the Krauts would keep airfields extended out as far as possible from the Father Land. Why not battle allied bombers from the coast. Oh well, their strategy is my gain.

FLAK, the Germans are tenacious when it comes to that. The formation wades into yet another black cloud of death. The edge of the barrage is like a curtain that the bombers pass through. It is nasty in here, a white flash and the appearance of a black puff of smoke marks the flight of an 88mm shell.

Nick starts juking across the sky as the Germans throw up an intense barrage. Their intent is to saturate the sky with flying pieces of hot steel. A sky full of shrapnel maximizes the chances of bringing a bomber down. We finally emerge from the black, man made cloud of destruction into a clear blue sky.

Laddy calls out, "Bandits." There they are. I see them in the distance. They are out of range, but I still issue my customary challenge. I lead the bandits and guesstimate the best I can. I let loose a couple of rounds. The tracers arc across the sky in the direction of the German fighters. "Hi bastards, I see you."

Four minutes later, I get my reply as the Huns tear through the formation in a head on pass. I keep the turret straight back and the guns level. This is my central starting point. I turn, aim and fire off quick bursts as the Krauts suddenly come into my field of vision. They zoom off into the distance tailed by tracers. It happens in an instant.

I usually keep my guns trained where a Kraut fighter has just past. I continue to pop off short bursts. I know nine times out of ten a wing man will be trailing the leader.

That is exactly what happens this time. I fire at the lead Kraut as he suddenly comes into view. My tracers fall short as the plane passes by. I squeeze off two more short bursts into the empty sky. The trailing Me-109 walks right into my rounds. I watch tracers smack into the fuselage of the trailing Tin Can.

The two fighters continue out of range. The lead fighter joins up with the gaggle of Me-109s as they prepare for another attack. The plane I hit leaves a thin trail of black smoke as it continues into the clouds below.

Leslie Lee and Hansen have to have nerves of steel. They play the ultimate chicken game. They watch the fighters come in head on. They watch twelve fighters, lined up abreast, barrel straight for them. They steel themselves to the perilous situation. They watch the flashes on the wings and noses as the Krauts start firing their guns. Once the Germans are in range, they fire back. All they can do is hope the Hun is a lousy shot.

The Krauts hope the same as they close on the bombers. Every forward firing gun in the formation opens fire. It must look like the whole sky is shooting at them. It's not over after the aerial game of chicken. They can get blasted passing through the formation.

That's exactly what happens. Laddy leads two Huns passing through in trail position. His shots rake the lead plane from cockpit to tail. No smoke, but the Me-109 snaps into violent barrel rolls. It corkscrews towards the earth until it breaks up. Laddy's gun camera will confirm that kill.

Another one of the 453rd's Liberators falls victim to the Hun. It lags behind and starts to lose altitude. The bomber falls back until it is out of sight. The B-24 looked fine, but there is obviously something wrong.

Holy Christ, two bombers across the formation just collided. One is upside down. The other has most of its starboard wing missing. They tumble, careening into each other as they plummet to the ground. The disintegrating fuselages shower pieces across the blue. Tumbling wings spew fuel into the sky. It could have been human error or mechanical failure. It could have been battle damage. Who knows, but they are gone. Nobody is getting out.

Leslie reports, "smoke pots" as we approach the I.P. The Krauts lay down a smoke screen next to the target. It is an attempt to spare the airfield. Not today, the target lays exposed under a shifting wind.

The attack is driven home. Leslie reports, "Bombs away." The airbase is swept under by general-purpose bombs. They walk across the runway in an instant. The strike looks good. We will know how the attack faired after a photo recon mission.

Another Liberator's wounds have finally turned fatal. She is on fire and falling back. Smoke from the port wing draws a line across the sky. Guys start to bail out; they are little specks that appear next to the plane. They slowly fall away from the stricken bomber.

This B-24 holds steady as more men bail out. The pilot must have put the bomber on auto pilot. The final count is ten men out. Parachutes dot the sky. The stricken B-24 straggles behind the formation slowly falling back. It finally erupts into a brilliant, crimson fireball. The explosion leaves only pieces behind. I hope I never have to bail out.

Luther calls out, "Enemy fighters!" The Krauts line up abreast and come tearing through again. Two more B-24s on the far side of the formation go down in the melee. The Huns regroup and press the attack. Guns pop off burst after burst as Penny defends herself. A Tin Can erupts into flames as it roars past on my left. Wow, it happens so fast. Hansen asks for a confirmation. "I see it," I reply.

Finally, the Germans streak through the formation for the last time. Where are those Mustangs? The formation flies home alone. A quick glance brings the welcomed sight of the Carter crew flying next to us. Thank God for one constant in this crazy life. I hope we all make it. By my count, we lost six bombers.

We are with the main group as we come home to Station #144. The stragglers will come later. We fly a holding pattern until it is our turn to land. Nick flares Penny out as we touch down. With a squeal of the tires, we are back home. Penny is brought to her hardstand, and the propellers slowly wind down to a halt.

There will be six ground crews that will have empty hardstands. Sixty men were lost. To watch the ground crews of lost bombers is a sad sight. They stand around with nothing to do. They walk over to the next hardstand to talk with that crew. What else can they do? They have lost their men and plane.

These ground crews will have to start over again. They will have to make bonds with a new crew. They will have to learn the quirks of their new plane. They will have to deal with the memory of their lost crew. They are ghosts for the ground crews, memories for the rest of their lives.

We get something to eat after we are debriefed. We fill the stove in our hut before we hit the sack. I put an entry in my diary after I trace this mission on the map. I thank God I made it. That was a rough one, but we got two kills. We fly again tomorrow.

#15; Alerted; April 10th; Tours, France: Airfield. We will be bombing an airfield. In briefing, we are told it will be another long one. Not the longest but long enough. We will be in the air six and a half hours.

The path of an air raid isn't always in a straight line. A formation may fly different directions for given amounts of time. This is done in hopes of confusing the enemy as to where the attack will take place. It is all in the name of giving the bombers a better chance of survival.

We go out to Penny and suit up. After everybody is aboard, Nick yells, "Clear on two." The engine coughs to life. Luther does the same on his side. As soon as all four engines are turning, they are run up. Everything checks out, we're good to go.

We taxi out and take our place in the line of silver and olive drab Liberators. We slowly move to the end of the runway. Nick does not stop as he turns our bomber onto the strip. With the throttles wide open, Penny races down the runway. Moments later, she lifts us into the sky.

Our bomber goes haywire as we fly a holding pattern over the Norfolk countryside. Half of the equipment has gone dead. The gauges show two dead batteries. Our pilots will not take any chances. Nick aborts and turns Penny around. The tower is radioed that we have electrical problems.

As soon as the last plane clears the runway, Nick brings Penny in. He taxis her to the hardstand at a high idle. We stay in the plane as our ground crew quickly changes out the troublesome batteries. With a thumbs up, we are sent on our way.

Penny rolls out again. We taxi to the head of an empty runway. Nick swings Penny on the strip without stopping. Our bomber screams down the runway at full power. Once again, we take to the skies. Nick climbs to the formation just as it turns for Tours. It was as simple as that.

We have Mustangs escorting us today. Yes sir, this is what I like. We cross into Hitler's France. Where are those dirty Kraut fighters now? Not one to be seen while the Mustangs are with us. They cruise along flying top cover. The P-51s are a great deterrent but they are no help when it comes to the anti-aircraft.

Angry black bursts start to fill the sky. BANG, a burst comes out of nowhere. Penny takes a hit, but all seems well. The same cannot be said looking to my right.

A B-24 in our box is hit. The starboard wing burns fiercely. It is beyond me how fuel can ignite in this thin air. The crew has to get out now. The bomber continues to lose altitude as it falls back. The fire spreads across the wing. It's only a matter of time before it explodes. Guys start bailing out. Nine little black specks fall away from the plane. The pilot has done his part, he better get out now. The bomber disappears in the distance.

The escorts go to work after we emerge from the barrage. The Mustangs turn into the approaching bandits. Go get em, boys! I once again witness dogfights to the death. Two Mustangs gang up on a Tin Can. They hook onto the tail of the Me-109 easily. This Kraut pilot is lousy.

He is going to get killed. Before a shot is fired, it's over. The pilot rolls the Me-109 on its back and falls out. There must have been a green son-of-a-bitch in that Tin Can.

The Me-110s don't want any of this action. They bug out at first sight of the escorts. That's right boys; keep those Krauts off our backs. The dogfight persists in the distance as the formation makes its run on the target.

Leslie reports, "Bombs away" as Penny lurches upward. The formation walks its bombs right down the runway. When the smoke clears, the airfield will be a cratered mess.

After the Mustangs drive the Huns off, they return to shepherd us home. A P-51 slowly pulls up alongside Penny. What a piece of machinery. The pilot looks us over, what a lucky bastard he is. The Mustangs dance around us in the midday sun.

We fly out of enemy territory unopposed. The formation crosses the channel under the protection of our fighters. Thank God for fighters.

Our escorts peel off over the coast of England. The group follows landmarks home over the East Anglican countryside. Things are starting to turn green below. Nice weather is around the corner. We get into a racetrack pattern as we wait our turn to land. Fifteen minutes later, we are taxiing to the hardstand.

That was some mission. Who knows what the results would have been without the escorts. We finish our smokes as we ride down the flight line to debriefing.

The interrogators know the questions to ask each man. They know what is relevant and what isn't. Everybody waits until each other is done. We drop off our flight bags before we head to the mess hall. It's time to unwind over a good supper. Talk centers around the P-51s.

Oh yes, to be a fighter pilot! The Mustang is a handsome machine. It is made by North American. It has an inline engine and a high flow wing, similar to the B-24's. This wing gives the P-51 maneuverability. It had limitations until the British mated a Rolls-Royce Merlin engine, and a four bladed paddle propeller to it. These modifications made the plane what it is. It is fast, has long range and possesses a great climb rate.

The P-51 has a greenhouse canopy but the latest variants are getting a bubble canopy. The plane carries four .50 caliber machine guns that deal out destruction. When carrying wing tanks, the Mustang can go with us just about anywhere. Its most recognizable feature is the radiator scoop under the fuselage between the wings.

The P-47 Thunderbolt wouldn't be a bad one to fly either. Republic builds them. It is a big fighter. It has a big old Pratt and Whitney radial engine that chews up the sky. It looks fat on certain angles but it is an excellent dogfighter at altitude. It is faster than the P-51 and it dives like a brick. I never saw anything get away from it. Look the hell out when a Thunderbolt dives.

With eight .50 caliber machine guns, it is a devastating gun platform. It has a greenhouse canopy but it too will be getting a bubble canopy. The P-47 can take a ton of abuse and it excels at ground attack. One of the P-47's names is Juggernaut, Jug for short. The Krauts call it Jabo.

The Lockheed P-38 Lightning is the one I like. The Germans avoid it, they call it the Fork-Tailed Devil. It is a twin-engine fighter. The inline engines are housed in their own booms. The booms connect with the stabilizer. The cockpit sits in its own fuselage between the two engines. It carries four .50 caliber machine guns and a 20 mm cannon in the nose.

It has a framed bubble canopy with a good field of vision all around. The P-38 has a problem power-diving though. The plane wants to tear itself apart. *(Unknown to the designers, the Lightning experienced compression problems as it neared the sound barrier in power dives.)* It is a big fighter, but it does its job well.

The guys conversation drones on in the background. I just daydream and laugh to myself. Fighters,...Mustangs, ...Thunderbolts,...Lightnings,...lucky bastards.

April 14th, the crews that flew the Berlin raids are called to muster. A few of them will not attend; they are dead. We are ordered to attention as our superior officers stand before us. Major Stewart informs the gathered crews, "You are receiving the Air Medal for the March 6th and 8th raids on Berlin." After a short ceremony, we are awarded our citations. We are saluted and dismissed.

#16; Alerted; April 18th; Tutow, Germany: Arado aircraft factory. We will be bombing an aircraft factory today. This will be an eight hour mission. We are told this factory makes jet aircraft. We must stop that kind of stuff on the ground. The Krauts get jets up in the air, it's bad news for all of us. The Mustang will be out classed.

A quick trip is made to the latrine before the Duce and Half carries us out to the hardstand. Penny's tail has a new paint job. The Air Corps has changed the tail markings of all the bomb groups. They will be color coded now.

All 453rd aircraft will have a white diagonal stripe that goes through a black painted outer tail surface. The radio call letters will be painted black inside the white stripe. The bombers painted like this look nice. The roundels with a big J will be phased out.

Luther climbs up on the flight deck and unlocks the controls. Nick does his walk around before he gets in the pilot's seat. We position our gear as our pilots go through the preflight checklist. After a smoke, the crew climbs into our bomb laden Liberator. Nick starts the engines and runs them up to reveal any problems. All the gauges check normal. The crew chief pulls the chocks that set Penny free. Our pilot releases the parking brake, and we are on our way.

We taxi off the hardstand onto the ramp. It is exciting every time, sitting among idling four engine machines of war. The B-24 in front of us turns on the runway and he is off. Nick waits 30 seconds before he takes our Liberator down the strip. With a nudge of the yoke, Penny leaps into the sky. We take our place in the lead element. Nick trims the plane as we turn for the enemy coast.

The formation pulls contrails as we cross the Zuyder Zee. There are always fishing trawlers below. They are pickets. They warn the Luftwaffe when we are coming. FLAK and fighters will be waiting for us.

We can bomb radar sites all day, it would not make a difference. Our movements are tracked a myriad of ways. Besides the trawlers, there are radio intercepts, spies, lookouts, you name it.

I have a bad feeling. I peer intently into the sky as we cross into enemy territory. Oh no, specks appear on the horizon. My guns are brought to bear on the distant, unidentified aircraft. Wait, wait for positive identification. They are Mustangs, it is not like a few months ago. I have to wait and make sure now. I cannot assume it's only Krauts up here anymore.

Under the protection of the escorts, the formation cruises five miles above enemy territory. After the fighters have reached their limit, they peel off to let another group take us the rest of the way. With a waggle of the wings, the Mustangs are gone. The escorts that are supposed to rendezvous with us are nowhere to be seen. I feel naked without them.

Five hours into the mission, there isn't any FLAK or enemy fighters to be seen. We approach the target in a crystal clear sky. The formation turns on the I.P to begin its run. I wait for the FLAK that never comes. Not one enemy aircraft appears. Leslie announces, "Bomb bay doors opened." Penny lurches upward as Leslie reports, "Bombs away." The formation does a wheel turn for home. The sky remains clear. No FLAK or fighters yet.

There are not any escorts to be seen. Nobody has come to cover us. We fly the return leg alone. It feels lonely way up here, so far from home.

As "Lucky Penny" cruises at 28,000 feet, a single fighter is spotted at 11 o'clock high. This plane is so high it is hard to tell what it is. The sun reflecting off its silver body makes it hard to identify.

All right, it's a P-47 Thunderbolt. It has a black and white checkered nose. He is really up there. The lone fighter cruises high above the formation in the bright blue sky. The sun dances across the Thunderbolt's wings and propeller. What is he doing up there all alone? KABLAM, the P-47 explodes into pieces.

WOW, it takes a moment for the mind to register what just happened. There is nothing to say. There is no rhyme or reason. I don't know what happened. There isn't any FLAK or fighters. The P-47 just blew up. It must have been catastrophic failure. Supercharger, who knows? Who was he? The remains of the Thunderbolt fall in the distant sky like so much confetti, strange.

There isn't any FLAK or fighters to contend with on the return leg. What more could I want? I wish all the missions could be like this. The formation breaks down over East Anglia. Each bomb group starts flying circuits over their base. We circle Old Buck until it's our turn to land. We touch down and taxi to the hardstand.

Everybody lights up as we get out of our flight gear. There is much speculation over the lone Thunderbolt. This topic is discussed all the way to debriefing. The strange incident is relayed to the interrogators. Well, they will find out who that was. The checkered nose belongs to some fighter group.

After a good dinner, it's off to the hut. A letter from Helen lifts my spirits. Missions like this make me believe I can make it. I will not fool myself though. I am dead, I just don't know it. I pray that I am wrong and thank God for protecting us again.

#17; Alerted; April 30th; Siracourt, France: Invasion coast, construction of installations. We will be attacking hardened targets. Penny will be loaded with eight 1,000 pound bombs. We are reminded that there is always the possibility of FLAK and fighters. The mission should be a milk run, but one never can tell. We decide to take the dog with us on this one.

After the briefing, we stop by the hut to grab the dog.

His oxygen mask and jacket are tossed in a parachute bag with the rest of the gear. Hansen lifts the dog up onto Turwilliger's lap before he hops on the truck.

Penny inquisitively sniffs the air as we ride down the flight line. Once at the hardstand, the dog watches us prepare for the mission. He curiously noses through the gear scattered about. Everybody gives our good luck charm a pet before they climb into the bomber. Laddy grabs him and takes him up through the bomb bay.

Everybody knows it's against regulations to have this dog on the plane. The brass knows aircrews occasionally take mascots up, but nothing is said.

Penny's engines cough and stumble as Nick and Luther bring the bomber to life. The dog happily sniffs the bomber floor indifferent to the sounds around him. He has done this before.

The engines are run up, everything checks out. Nick sets the powerful radials at idle, then taxis out. Laddy sets the dog on his lap as we get into takeoff positions. Nick takes us down the runway into a strong head wind. Moments later, we are off.

We fall in on the edge of the formation. Laddy hands our mascot to Turwilliger. Laddy then prepares to get into his turret. The dog excitedly wags his tail as he watches the crew in action. Victor puts the dog's fleece jacket on in the falling temperature. Once we reach altitude, our mascot's oxygen mask is put on. The length of his hose limits his movement; the dog curls up on his blanket next to the oxygen feed.

I am accepting what intelligence tells us as good information. This is supposed to be a milk run so I go to the flight deck. If we get attacked, we could be in trouble. I am taking a chance. Hansen works his turret while Joe Craft listens at his radio. Nick and Luther know what they are doing. The plane practically flies itself the way they have it trimmed.

The formation forges ahead. The bombers wings above us spread out blocking the sun. They cast a shadow on "Lucky Penny." The silver-bodied B-24s take on a bluish hue as they mirror the sky around them. I get the sensation of just how high we are.

I watch the tail gunners of the planes in front of us search the skies, something I should be doing. Ball turrets begin to emerge from under the bombers. They appear as giant eyeballs rotating in the sky. Laddy is crazy. He has to be nuts to hang out from under an airplane. His ass is literally hanging in the wind.

The planes do look majestic in their flight. The formation pulls contrails for just a moment as we break into a different temperature layer. Turbulence causes a plane to occasionally dip a wing as we soar through the heavens.

In the distance, other combat boxes can be seen. The lower elements are silhouetted against a blanket of clouds. The silver B-24s toss a glare as the sun reflects off their shiny bodies. The olive drab bombers stand out in stark contrast against a white backdrop. Our formation is insignificant in a vast sky.

Nick tells me to get to my station as we near the enemy coast. I give our dog a pat on the head as I go to my turret. Nothing to report as the formation approaches the target area. No FLAK or fighters to be seen.

The group turns on the I.P. The attack begins. The lead B-24 drops its marker bomb. The smoke trail can clearly be seen with the payload. Leslie reports, "Bombs away." The formation lurches up in unison. We turn onto the heading that will take us home. The sky is clear. I like this. I hope it stays this way until we get back.

Once we are clear of the enemy coast, I return to the flight deck. When it's just the crew, Nick is one of us. He tells Luther, "Take over for awhile." Nick lets go of the yoke and starts talking about flying. He tells us how he wanted to be a fighter pilot, but he was told he was too old. He calls aft to check on the dog, all is O.K. After awhile, he tells me to check the fuel transfer lines. These are located on the bulkhead in the bomb bay. They have a tendency to leak. It is a quirk with the B-24. The fuel lines check out O.K.

Nick takes control of Penny as we cross the English

coast. There is a huge build-up of troops and equipment below. I know the invasion; the big one will be coming. The question is when?

We approach Station #144 under a partly cloudy sky. Nick tells Luther to set the flaps as they put Penny on final approach. Nick calls out, "Landing gear down." Luther hits the lever. The indicators read good. Luther replies, "Landing gear locked."

Final approach brings us over the fence where the kids stand waving like mad. Nick flares Penny out as we touch the ground. Nick puts the engine settings back to idle as we coast down the strip.

The bomb bay doors are opened as we taxi to the hardstand. Once Penny is parked, the cowl flaps are opened and all the switches are flipped off. After the parking brake is set, the controls are locked. Finally, the flight deck is cleared.

The dog emerges from under Penny with the crew. He wanders among the guys. He investigates each parachute bag as we get out of our gear. We enjoy a smoke as we wait for the truck to take us to debriefing.

When the truck arrives, everybody throws their gear aboard. Last but not least, Victor lifts the dog onto the truck. We tell the driver to stop by the shack so we can drop the dog off before we debrief.

That was the easiest mission I ever flew. There wasn't any enemy to speak of. I wish it could always be this way. Our Liberator now has seventeen bombs and seven kills painted on her.

#18; Alerted; May 1st; Invasion Coast; Watten, France: Rocket installations. We are awakened at 1 A.M. and briefed. We will strike rocket installations on the French coast. The Krauts have been blasting London with them; they must be destroyed. We will be carrying four 2,000 pound bombs. We will be hitting hardened targets for sure. We are informed Lightnings will be escorting us today. That's fine with me.

After we get our chutes, we ride out to the plane. We prepare for the mission in the predawn darkness. Nick and Luther go through the checklist as the rest of the crew has a smoke. Everybody climbs aboard when Nick is ready to fire Penny up.

Fire jumps from the exhaust pipes as the engines are started one by one. Soon flames continuously leap from the pipes of steadily idling engines. Everything looks good. After I climb aboard, Nick closes the bomb bay doors behind me.

Penny's landing lights lead the way off the hardstand. Nick follows the B-24 ahead of us. He works the throttles as we turn onto the strip. Huge flames erupt from the exhaust as we race down the runway. At the right moment, Nick puts the spurs to Penny. Our bomber leaps into the predawn sky.

The 453rd turns for France under the dawn of a new day. Boats patrolling the channel cast long shadows in the early morning light. The P-38s join us as we approach the enemy coast.

A lone B-24 carrying the 453rd's markings is spotted in the distance. What is he doing out there? He doesn't have any support from the other bombers. This Liberator is not making any kind of an attempt to join the formation. Radio contact cannot be made. This B-24 shadows us. The P-38s turn to investigate this lone bomber. The Liberator peels off before positive identification can be made.

I know what's going on. The Germans are shadowing our formation with a captured bomber. They follow the planes and radio back formation size, speed and direction. This gives the Luftwaffe time to plot out an effective defense. This bomber vanishes like a ghost into the early morning sky.

The FLAK ahead sends chills down my spine. How many times can a guy go into this stuff and make it out? A dread feeling comes over me as we approach the target. Near misses rock Penny. CRUMPH, WHAM, Penny shudders but she keeps going. CRUMPH, CRUMPH, the bursts are intense and accurate. There are some good gunners down there. CRUMPH, CRUMPH, I don't like this at all. The formation defiantly flies through the black cloud that tries to bring it down.

Nick starts swinging in and out on the edge of the element. It doesn't seem to help. This is it, we are going to die. We are going down today. We'll be finished before we start the bomb run.

Flying straight and level make us sitting ducks. We are easy pickings. I can only cringe in my turret as the FLAK batters the formation. Penny lurches upward as our bombs fall free. Let's get the hell out of here! The formation turns away for home.

I always have a ringside seat in Penny's tail. The 2,000 pound bombs cannot be missed as they fall. I watch them until they disappear from sight. Moments later, KABLAM. Huge shock waves emanate from the center of violent explosions. WOW, I don't know if those bombs did anything, but it impressed the hell out of me.

CRUMPH, the FLAK snaps me back to the dire situation I am in. It does not stop. Come on guys; get us out of range of this stuff. All I can do is cower as we wade through this evil, black cloud. The bombers trailing us take evasive action. They put space between each other as they look for a way out of this airborne hell.

We finally break into a clear sky. Shadowy objects that are bombers emerge from the dark cloud behind us. The formation frees itself of this sinister barrage. The man made cloud of death shrinks in the distance.

It's hard to believe, but it looks like all the planes have made it. The bombers fly home under the protection of the Lightnings.

Over the North Sea, Hansen reports that the fuel transfer lines are leaking. We could light off at any moment. The fuel leaks down the bulkhead and across the bomb bay doors. Nothing, nothing can be done to stem the flow. Static electricity or a spark and it's all over. We fly a good two hours with fuel leaking into the bomb bay.

We radio our situation as we approach Old Buck. We

will be one of the first planes to land. We only make one lap over the base before Nick brings Penny in. As soon as we get off the runway, Nick opens the bomb bay doors. Our B-24 leaves a thin trail of fuel down the ramp.

Nick quickly parks Penny at the hardstand. Nobody wants any of this. Everybody gets the hell out before the propellers come to a complete stop. The crew jogs/runs until they are a safe distance from the plane.

The fuel transfer lines leak like a sieve. A puddle of high octane fuel grows under Penny. The smell of petrol permeates the air. Nick and Luther work fast shutting Penny down; they hurriedly join us clear of the plane.

I can't believe we made it. We survived all that FLAK and the broken fuel lines. Boy, I sweated this one hard. I am spent; it's hard to believe how a mission can drain you. We refrain from smoking as we get out of our flight gear.

Despite the leaking fuel, the ground crew tallies the unofficial shrapnel count. There are 20 holes in Penny.

When am I going to get it? I can't keep playing this game and coming back. Major Stewart shouts out in passing, "How was it, Black Fury?" I reply, "Good sir, we made it." With a smile and a nod, Major Stewart drives over to Penny's officers.

We tell the story of the lone B-24 shadowing the formation at debriefing. When we are finished, we grab a bite in the mess hall. What a day. I am starved, Thank God we made it. We have two weeks off and I plan on shacking up with my gal.

Nick joins us in the mess hall. He tells me I can fly my make up mission tomorrow. It sounds good to me. I have to catch up so I can finish with the guys. After the doc checks my frostbite, I head to the hut. I get my map out and trace today's mission path. I write an entry in my diary before I hit the rack. I silently pray until I drift off.

Alerted; May 2nd; Siracourt, France: Rocket installations. This is my make up mission. I just want to get it out of the way. I don't want to be separated from the guys. I grab my flight gear and meet the other crew in front of their barracks. The waist gunner is sick so I will take his place. I introduce myself before we go to briefing.

We will be hitting the invasion coast once more. It is rocket installations again. The 453rd will fly as decoys on this one. No bombs will be carried. We will carry this stuff called Chaff instead.

This Chaff is like aluminum foil that is cut in long thin strips. At a certain point in the mission, we are to throw this stuff out the windows. It is supposed to confuse the German radar. Its intended purpose is to give the Krauts false images on their radar screens. The Germans will not know where the real attack is coming from because of this. They will not be able to scramble fighters or move FLAK carts in advance.

We will be part of a ruse that veils the intentions of the real attack. The 453rd will throw this Chaff into the sky and create a ghost formation. The real attack will then fly on to the target … I am told.

After we grab our parachutes, we ride out to the hardstand. We gear up as the pilot gets his B-24 ready to go. I climb up through the bomb bay to make my way aft. Recent events compel me to examine the bulkhead for faulty fuel lines. Everything looks good.

A hop on the catwalk takes me through the rear bulkhead of the B-24. A step around the turret well puts me in the waist gunner position. The waist gunner points to the gun I will be on. I swing the .50 cal. from side to side in a cursory check.

Satisfied with my gun, my attention is turned to the cardboard boxes of this Chaff that line the sides of the fuselage. I open one and put my hand in. It looks like tin foil; the material is light and metallic in appearance. All the strips are cut the same length and width. They are obviously this way for a reason. Whatever it is supposed to do, there is an awful lot of it.

The pilots start the engines as our discussion continues aft. They are run up and returned to idle. The control surfaces are exercised, everything looks good. The chocks are pulled, and we are off. We taxi down the ramp to the head of the runway.

Everybody assumes takeoff positions. A signal flare arcs across the sky and the 453rd starts taking flight. When we reach the runway, we swing onto it without stopping. This is done so no forward momentum is lost. The pilot pushes the throttles wide open. We hurl down the strip gathering speed. With a slight pull on the yoke, we are off. We climb to take our place in the formation.

These guys seem alright. I hope they are a good crew. I swing the .50 cal. back and forth. I angle it down to sight in the bomber off our wing through the crosshairs. I lead the B-24 as imaginary rounds hammer the cockpit.

I charge the Ma Duce as we cross the channel. Oxygen masks go on as we climb into the rarified air. Throat mics are checked, everything is in working order. We cross the coast of France five miles above our enemy.

The pilot tells us to get ready. We drag a few boxes of the Chaff to our positions and wait. On the pilots command, we start throwing handfuls of it out the waist gunner windows. We empty box after box. As soon as a box is emptied, it is slid aside to make room for another. Handfuls of Chaff are thrown out the windows. The surrounding bombers do the same.

The sky starts to fill with this stuff. It looks like a foil snowstorm. This Chaff is everywhere. It slides off the surrounding bombers as it gently floats across the sky. The group makes a huge cloud of this stuff. It is miles long. This aluminum cloud sparkles in the sky as the sun dances across the metallic strips.

CRUMPH, the sky fills with black puffs of exploding 88mm shells. Fear drives us to start throwing the Chaff out the windows faster. CRUMPH, CRUMPH, the boxes are hastily lifted in the windows and the metallic strips are shaken out into the slipstream. It is a furious attempt to get this stuff in the sky quickly.

This frenzied situation takes a comical turn. We begin to laugh at each other's frantic actions. Boxes of Chaff are hurriedly shaken out the windows amid whoops and laughter. The faster we throw this stuff out, the better our chances are of getting out of this alive. The sky takes on the appearance of a gigantic, silver, blizzard.

After this Chaff is pitched into the sky, the formation turns to another heading. We fly this bearing for a while, then change direction again. The real attack formation follows a different route while the phantom formation is carried on the wind. To the German radar, it looks like three separate attacks. German forces cannot be massed for a defense. Where is the real attack? The indecision buys the real raid time.

We turn back to England as the attack formation continues to the target. The group is not harassed as we journey home. Laughter erupts again as the waist gunner and I look at each other. It feels good to laugh. This Chaff, it's a hell of a thing.

When the formation returns, the group starts flying circuits over Norfolk. After five minutes, the pilot brings us in. The kids wave to us as we cross over the fence on final approach. I lean out the waist position and wave back. The kids wave fervently in acknowledgement. It is fun.

With a squeal of the tires, we touchdown and rollout to the end of the strip. Once on the hardstand, the engines are shut down. I emerge with my one time crew from under the bomber. Everybody is elated in the knowledge that they have survived another mission.

We discuss the virtues of this Chaff as we get out of our flight gear. It was a milk run for the most part. The mission went well. The 453rd did not have any losses. The Duce and Half takes us to debriefing. When everybody is finished, we leave the building together. With a shake of hands, I tell the guys ,"See ya around."

I laugh to myself as I take a leisurely walk to the hut. I am surprised to see the guys are still here. I thought they would be gone on leave. They pretend they do not notice me as I walk in the door. It doesn't last long, crooked smiles crack across their faces. They are glad to see me. Yes, they waited for the planes to come in. I now have the same amount of missions as the rest of the crew. We will finish or die together.

May 8th, while on furlough, we learn "Lucky Penny" has been shot down. Our girl is gone. The plane that took us from the U.S.A. to Waller Field was blown out of the sky. The plane that saved us over Siracourt is gone. The plane that I got my kill over Gotha in, is lost. The plane that brought us home, time after time, is no more.

What happened? "Lucky Penny" was shot down over Brunswick, Germany. No survivors. It figures, somebody else takes her and look what happens. Those bastards lost our plane. It probably never would have happened if we were flying her. We knew how to treat our girl.

The ground crew waited but Penny didn't come back. Our ground crew took the lonely walk to the next hardstand to lend a hand. They lost a plane, but not a crew.

At least we are alive. We were fortunate to be on leave. Then again, if we were flying her, would she have been shot down? Penny was lucky for us to the end. Our trusty, olive drab mount is gone. The dirty, rat bastard Krauts got her. We will have a new plane to break in by the time we finish our furlough.

#19; Alerted; May 13th; Tutow, Germany: Focke Wolf aircraft plant. This will be a long ride. We are going to strike the nest of the Butcher Bird. I don't like those Fw-190s. We hear the dreaded words, expect FLAK and fighters. At least we will have fighter escorts to deal with enemy aircraft. P-47s and P-51s will be riding shotgun. That is fine with me.

We truck out to the hardstand. There she is, the new Penny. We were out to her earlier but I am still impressed. She is a shiny aluminum Liberator. She is a J model. The serial number of our new aircraft is 42-95312. We have the black painted tail with a white diagonal stripe painted through it. All the other identification letters and numbers remain the same.

Boy, quite a few of the olive drab B-24s are gone. Some of the survivors still retain the white roundels. Well, they may have got our plane, but they didn't get us. The ground crew walks around with us as we check the new Penny out again.

Nick nods his head in approval as he examines the armor plates bolted beneath the cockpit canopy. Ah, yes, the ground crew has already painted "Lucky Penny" on the nose. It isn't finished, though, the Roman numeral two is outlined in chalk, but it isn't painted in. The name "Lucky Penny" is painted black on an upward angle between the nose and cockpit. Nick wants it on both sides this time. We have our bombs and kills painted under the cockpit. We will write our names under the top turret the next time we are down.

Powell gathers us in front of the plane so he can take a picture. After that, he tells our ground crew to get in front of Penny with us. Powell grabs a passing enlisted man to take a picture of everybody.

We are told the new Penny is ready to go. We are reminded to take care of her. I get our good luck doll and prop him up next to my turret. Nick and Luther begin the starting sequence. The engines cough to life one by one. Soon all the engines settle to an idle.

Nick and Luther act like they are in a new Cadillac as we taxi out. We fall into the rolling procession of bombers. Nick grins as he works the throttles. The bomber ahead of us turns onto the runway and it's gone. About 30 seconds later, we go. Nick rolls onto the strip without stopping. As soon as Penny is straight, the mighty radial engines are gunned to full throttle.

Nick pulls the yoke back a touch when Penny reaches 130 miles per hour. In an instant, we are airborne. "Gear up," Nick calls out. Luther hits the lever to raise the landing gear. Luther slowly raises the flaps as we gain speed and altitude. We take to the skies in our new bomber.

We climb to join the circling planes. The 453rd falls in behind its rally ship. We follow "Wham Bam" to the groups position in the formation. Once we are set in place, the rally ship leaves. "Wham Bam" will fly circuits over the North Sea and relay radio messages back to Old Buck. The attack force starts its journey to Europe.

After unlocking the turret, I give it a swing to the left. All clear. This turret is some piece of machinery. I sit inside a plexiglas and metal bubble. It is built by Consolidated or contracted out to Vultee. The turret itself is hydraulically driven. Everything inside is powered by electricity. The inside of the turret is green in color. The color is called zinc chromate. The seat is mounted between two .50 caliber machine guns. They ride in cradles that rock up and down. The bullets are fed to the guns by feed tracks that run inside the fuselage. Once a bullet is fired, the spent shell falls into an ejector chute under the turret. The shell is discarded, tumbling into the sky.

There is a panel of bulletproof glass mounted in front of my face. There is an armor plate below the glass. There are armor plates on each side of the seat. My flak jacket sits on the steel seat to protect my rear end.

The turret is controlled with a stick that looks like a broken T. The handles angle down on each side. The firing tit and gun sight controls are on these handles. If you push the control stick forward, the guns point down. If you pull it back, the guns point up. Turn the control stick left or right and the turret responds in a like manner.

The gun sight is mounted on a horizontal bar at face level. It is a reflector gun sight. This sight automatically calculates the lead and deflection of the target you are shooting at.

When you look through the sight, there is a pointer that acts as a fixed aiming point. This pointer tells you where the guns are aimed. Another pointer moves with the rotating of the handle on the control stick. You dial the moving pointer with the control stick until you have your target between the two pointers. The gun's sight calculates the lead and deflection at the same time. Once the target is dialed between the pointers, it is in the crosshairs, so to speak. That is when you fire your guns.

The outer surface of the turret is framed. The rear of the turret has two doors hinged to the frame. I had my doors removed. The framework holds the plexiglas panels that give the turret its shape. Some of the outer panels are tinted green to help with the sun. Who would think I would be sitting in something like this; flying over some country in Europe.

German fighters are spotted as they come up. Oh no, they are Focke Wolfs. Mustangs intercept them in the distance. Two P-51s drive a Fw-190 to the deck. The lead P-51 fires off a burst that hits home in the Krauts cockpit area. The pilot ejects the canopy from a burning cockpit.

The Kraut is too low to bailout. He jumps anyway. The Focke Wolf goes into a shallow high-speed dive. It cartwheels across the ground blossoming into a huge fireball. The whole mess tumbles across the deck in spectacular fashion. After destroying their prey, the Mustangs zoom climb to altitude.

This is a big raid. It reminds me of Berlin. By the time our group reaches the target, it is a seething mess below. Explosions erupt through the smoke obscured carnage. The industrial complex has layer upon layer of bombs dumped on it. With the words, "Bombs away," Penny adds to the destruction. We turn for home as the stream behind us continues to hammer the target.

No FLAK; there hasn't been any at all. The escorts have intercepted any German fighters that have come up. I hope it stays this way. Our fighters are the best. It was downright hair-raising before escorts could go all the way with us.

The only thing about the fighters that tick off the bomber crews is this. Air Command has seen it fit to give fighters credit when bomber crews get kills. Six times out of ten, the credit is given to an escorting fighter. They can't argue with a gun camera in a turret though. I can live with it as long as the escorts keep the Krauts off our backs.

We are not harassed as we cross the channel for home. The formation breaks down over East Anglia. Each group follows their rally ship to their respective base.

We drop out of the holding pattern and come in. Nick flares our B-24 out as we touch the ground. We roll onto our hardstand and park our new Liberator. So far, so good. Come on Penny II, I only have ten missions to go. I want to hang on. I want to believe I am not dead.

After dinner, I read my mail. My brother had joined the Army Air Corps. He had become a radio operator in a B-24. He was flying with the 98th Bomb Group out of Italy. They are called the Pyramiders. He was shot down and is now a prisoner of war. The Red Cross told my mom he is alive and alright. My brother is in a P.O.W. camp in Germany.

Oh boy, at least he is alive. My mom must be worried sick. Both her boys are off fighting. I will have to kill him if we survive the war. I pray hard until I fall asleep.

#20; Alerted; May 15th; Siracourt, France: Coastal installations. It will be a four hour mission. We will be hitting hardened targets again. Something is up; we are always hitting these coastal targets. The invasion has to come, but I'm not really sure where. We repeatedly attack targets along the coast of France. The invasion could land in any of these areas that we hit over and over. Then again, these missions could be nothing more than decoys. Who knows? I just want to make it home.

After we get our parachutes, we climb in the back of the truck. Nobody tries to fool anybody anymore with false bravado. We fear for our lives. There is small talk, but inside we are getting ready to climb in that plane.

I assume I am dead as we pull up to Penny II. I put my gear on wondering if this plane is going to be my coffin today. Is this my fate? Do I die in this big, fat piece of aluminum? Nick and Luther disappear into the cockpit to start the preflight checklist. The crew climbs aboard before the engines are started.

I wait under Penny's wing as she comes to life. The roar of each engine is like a siren calling me to my fate.

They beckon me into the plane. Will it be my last ride? I duck beneath Penny and grudgingly climb aboard.

Is this the last time I taxi down this ramp? Is this where my life ends? What about all the sunny days to come? Do I die half way around the world? Do I die five miles up in the sky somewhere between heaven and earth?

Penny swings on the runway and we are off. We form up and head out over the channel.

It is cold at 28,000 feet. It is 40 below zero up here. It is so cold my toes hurt. They are freezing. Powell reports we are entering enemy territory. Nick tells us to stay alert. No anti-aircraft or enemy fighters to be seen yet. I could get used to this.

Our escorts go on the hunt. Half the formation peels off and dives away. The P-47s go down to the deck to strafe targets of opportunity. The Thunderbolts dodge and weave across the landscape. The Jugs leave white puffs of smoke trailing behind their wings when they fire their guns. Sometimes I catch a glimpse of a fireball erupting from a building or train that has just been hammered by a P-47. I guess the Germans have no time for us. They are too busy dealing with the Thunderbolts.

It must be terrifying to have fighters suddenly appear out of nowhere. They come in at treetop level. They race towards you with guns blazing. The brave enemy gunner stands his ground and duels with the attacking fighters. The P-47s maul the target and are gone in a flash. The Jugs cut a swath of destruction in their paths. Those eight .50 caliber machine guns chew targets up.

Some of those fighter jocks are good or should I say, crazy. They come in so low their propellers are literally inches from the ground. This is called zero altitude attack. Enemy gunners have to look down at the P-47s as they go by. These pilots have crashed into telephone poles, hillsides, even houses. They damage their planes on trees and chimneys. They are sitting on hot seats and they know it. They are insane.

The sky is clear of anti-aircraft and fighters as we approach the target. Leslie watches for the lead bomber to drop its payload. Penny lurches up as Leslie announces, "Bombs away." The formation wheels home in a sky void of the enemy. We are not in the clear yet. We still have to get back. The formation flies the return leg unmolested.

The sun glints off the aluminum bombers that now fill the sky. All the B-24s that the group receives now come in their natural aluminum finish. Earlier in the war, the bombers were painted olive drab to camouflage them from the enemy as they sat on the ground. That was when the threat of an air raid was real. We now control the skies over England. There really is no point in painting them.

The white Cliffs of Dover come into view as the formation races across the channel. They are a sign of salvation for countless aircrews in crippled aircraft. An R.A.F. airfield lays just beyond them. God knows how many crews saw the cliffs as a beacon of hope, a chance for survival.

The sun feels good on my face as we fly over the English countryside. The trip from my turret to the flight deck stretches my numb legs. My feet tingle as we come in and park. I toss my gear out of the bomb bay and jump to the ground.

OOUCH, sharp pains shoot up my legs. My toes really hurt. I can't feel them when I wiggle them. I'm not stupid, these are the symptoms of frostbite. I immediately sit on the ground and take off my shoes and socks. My big toes do not look very good. I rub them to get the circulation flowing, they burn and sting to the touch.

Nick shakes his head with disapproval at the sight of me. He gives me hell about wearing my dress shoes instead of boots. He tells me to get my feet checked out after we debrief.

I will watch my toes. If they don't get better, I'll go see the flight surgeon. We debrief then go get something to eat. My toes burn and tingle as we sit around the table contemplating our chances of making thirty missions.

We sweat these missions hard anymore. We are starting to believe we may make it. I just don't want to get killed after all of this. I don't want to be too careful and get killed either.

My toes sting with every step I take. They feel like they are on fire as we head to our Nissen hut. At least we have the next two days off. I am beat. Even my throbbing toes cannot keep me awake.

At the crack of dawn, Laddy, Joe Craft and I go to breakfast. After we finish, we go down the road to pick up our clothes. Our favorite lady answers the door with a smile. She gladly invites us in. We trade rations for our clean laundry and give the boy some chocolate. We talk for a few moments then thank her. We tell her we will be back with more clothes on our next day off. We return to our barracks and square things away before we go to Attleboro.

KNOCK, KNOCK, KNOCK, KNOCK, KNOCK. Startled, everybody jumps. A bike slides down the side of our corrugated hut. Joe Craft pulls his .45 and takes aim at the wall. POW, POW, POW, he fires in the direction of the sound. Holes appear in our shack.

We snap at Joe. Holy Christ man, what the hell is wrong with you? Are you crazy? Are you trying to kill somebody? Joe Craft looks at us clearly pissed off until it sinks in what he just did. We run outside to look around. There is a bike leaning against the barracks, but there isn't anybody to be seen. As we inspect the area, we get some crooked looks from fellow airmen. Nothing comes of this but, man, oh man.

#21; Alerted; May 19th; Brunswick, Germany: Marshalling yards. We are briefed. Our target is rail yards. This will be an eight hour mission. There will be FLAK and fighters. We will have a fighter escort, that's music to my ears. Our escorts can't do anything about the FLAK though. My toes feel better; we'll see how it goes. I have to see how these newly issue boots work.

We have a smoke on our way to the parachute hanger.

We lay our stuff on the ground in front of us as we wait for our ride. With the usual fanfare, we climb aboard the truck. Our flight bags are tossed off the truck with disregard when we reach the hardstand. We hedge our chances as we go through our equipment. Nick and Luther then prepare to start Penny up.

The same routine is played out on hardstands across Old Buck. An engine coughs to life. Soon more engines join in. A cough turns into a roar. One here, then one there. One of Penny's engines joins the cacophony. The 453rd is coming to life. The drone of engines can be heard for miles.

A procession of bomb laden Liberators roll down the flight line. The ground trembles as they sit idling, at the end of the ramps. We wait for the signal to go. I poke my head out of the escape hatch to get a good look at the group. WOW what a sight!

Son-of-a-bitch, the wind just blew my ball cap off! Oh no, Helen's ribbon is pinned on it. There is no getting it now. Nick taps me on the leg and yells, "Close it up." We turn onto the runway and we are off.

I better not get killed now, I'm over half way. The safety pins are pulled from the bombs as we begin our journey over the channel. They are stuffed in my pocket before I continue aft.

Laddy is already in his turret. He hangs beneath Penny lazily scanning the sky. Victor and Turwilliger are looking out the same window at something below. I settle into my turret for the long mission. The skies are empty as the formation crosses the English Channel.

The FLAK starts as we approach the enemy coast. This anti-aircraft really puts a knot in my stomach. I can't do a thing about it. Praying I make it is all I can do. The FLAK barges moored in the channel create an angry black cloud that we have to fly through.

We aren't even over land yet and we have to deal with this FLAK. Penny is bounced by the bursts that try to bring her down. We press the attack. The formation loosens as we fly out of one barrage only to enter another. Some of them look like a black wall in the sky. The FLAK carts chase us across Europe. They hound us until we out pace them. We emerge from the barrage into a clear sky. Once again, our escorts are waiting.

The hours are spent praying in fear. I cringe on my seat as we enter one barrage after another. We finally approach the target. Our group follows the lead bomber's signal, "Bombs away." Moments later, the ground suddenly erupts. Bombs roll over the target. The marshalling yard is repeatedly wracked with salvos of high explosives.

The FLAK stops before we start our turn for home. This can only mean one thing and Leslie announces it, "Fighters out ahead." Me-109s, those son-of-a-bitchin Tin Cans.

The Me-109 is a small single-engine fighter. The Krauts pump them out like they are going out of style. They carry a 20 mm cannon in the nose and machine guns in the cowling in front of the cockpit. There must be 10 different variants of this airplane. The latest version has cannons mounted under the wings. They are nimble, but have trouble at the highest altitudes.

The Krauts hurl themselves at the formation with guns blazing. They streak through the bombers then they are gone. It always happens that fast. The closing speed is astounding. No bombers are mortally wounded in the first pass. The Germans form up again just out of range of our guns. The Me-109s fly parallel to the bombers as they prepare for another head on pass.

The Mustangs jump the Huns before they can get out ahead of the formation. Our escorts drive the Me-109s off. A dogfight erupts in the distance. The fighters pull contrails that run in every possible direction. They look like a child's scribbling in the sky. Go get them boys! Give those dirty Krauts hell.

We are targeted by FLAK once again. The 88mm cannons spit shells five miles into the sky. CRUMPH, CRUMPH, here we go again. All I can do is sit here and pray. We just have to survive this FLAK and get home.

It's not going to happen in the upper element. FLAK

claims another bomber. This B-24 begins to lag behind. A thin trail of black smoke comes off of the wing. Two engines are dead. The Liberator falls back until it is out of sight. Good luck to that crew. A straggler like that will be jumped and shot to pieces.

BLAM, a B-24 in our box takes a hit in the waist! The Liberator's skin is blown out and peeled back instantly by the slipstream. The force of the explosion blows the waist gunner out of the horrendous gash in the side of the plane. The two halves of the airman fall from the sky. His intestines uncoil between them as he plummets.

My God, the ball turret falls free. It gyrates wildly as it plunges earthward. It finally stabilizes with its guns pointing straight up. This guy has no hope. You cannot fit in the ball turret with a parachute. He is riding it all the way in.

What does a twenty year old guy think when he knows he is dead? What goes through a guys mind as he takes that two and a half minute ride to the ground?

What a horrific way to go. Does he watch the formation shrink away in the distance as he falls? Does he squint one last time as the sun shines in his eyes? Does a trapped guy accept his fate as he plunges to the earth? Does he just close his eyes and pray as he waits for impact? Does he cry as he thinks of a future without him? Does he scream in terror as he looks out at the sky? Does he get out his .45 and blow his brains out?

God only knows. I try to physically shake the thoughts out of my mind. The waist gunner and ball turret fall away until they are out of sight.

Not a word is spoken in Penny. Laddy's hair has to be standing on the back of his neck. The stricken bomber continues to fly. It stubbornly holds formation even with its aluminum side laid open. The green interior is clearly visible through the jagged, gaping hole. Barring catastrophic failure, the Liberator has a chance, as long as it can keep pace.

CRUMPH, CRUMPH, Penny jerks and shudders as a burst goes off nearby. We are alright. The engines sound fine. All the planes vibrations feel normal. Nick zig-zags on the edge of the element in his dance to avoid the anti-aircraft. This maneuver does work. Once again, brackets of FLAK go off where we should have been. Finally, we break free of the barrage. That was rough. I can't get the sight of that falling ball turret out of my mind.

The formation crosses over the Zuyder Zee. The FLAK barges open up again. Does this ever end? The formation drops in altitude as the bombers begin to circle back. Nick announces, "We are going to attack the FLAK barges." The bombers sweep in for a strafing run.

Crew 41 opens up on their tormenters. Penny vibrates as the .50 caliber machine guns spit out a steady stream of death. It's too easy. The .50s chew up the barges. The enemy gunners dive in the water for cover. The barges come into my field of view. Men scatter across the decks. Broken bodies lay strewn about.

I rake a barge from one end to the other. Krauts are blown apart and I don't care. Men and material fly everywhere as half-inch bullets destroy whatever they hit. The Krauts that dive into the sea disappear in huge spouts of water.

We are getting some payback. This is for all the FLAK we have faced. This is for every bomber shot down. The formation circles around again. Here you go, you son-of-a-bitches. Turwilliger lays on his trigger blasting a group of men. It looks like a meat grinder exploded into the sky. I curse out loud as I hose down a barge with hot lead. Once we get our revenge, the formation climbs for home.

I make my way to the flight deck as we fly into East Anglia. The wind howls into the cockpit through a shattered pane of the windshield. Nick has a gash on his face. He tells me it was close. A FLAK burst went off a little above and ahead of Penny. A piece of shrapnel shattered one of the panes in front of him. He got a face full of glass. Luckily, he was wearing his oxygen mask and goggles.

The crippled planes land first as we fly a circuit over Old Buck. We hold this pattern until it is our turn to come in. With a squeal of the tires, our Liberator touches down.

Nick takes Penny to her hardstand. She was ridden hard, but she came through for us. Our pilots shut our trusty mount down.

Well, we are all back safe. We debrief before we get something to eat. Charlie the cook has always treated us well. Today, he comes and sits with us. He leans over and asks us in a whisper, "Can you guys get me a .45 pistol?" Right away Joe Craft replies, "Sure." He tells us thanks then brings us a plate of pork chops.

We leave the mess hall with full stomachs. Turwilliger grabs a bucket of coal and loads the stove before we hit the sack. We fly again tomorrow. Thanks to God, we all are safe.

#22; Alerted; May 20th; Reims, France: Marshalling yards. We are informed this will be a five hour mission, not too bad. We will be hitting marshalling yards again. I study the map as we are briefed. We are told we will have fighter escorts. It will be Lightnings. It is only a matter of time until I hear the words I hate, expect FLAK and fighters.

Flight gear in hand, we walk out into the early morning air. My toes are feeling better, these new boots feel great. No more shoes for me. First, it's my face, now it's my toes.

We pull Victor aboard as the truck leaves for the hardstand. We are dropped off just as the ground crew finishes turning the propellers. Nick and Luther go up to the flight deck to start the checklist.

Soon enough, the engines come to life. We taxi out to the end of the ramp. Nick runs the engines up one last time for a final check. Flaps are set for takeoff as we wait our turn. Thirty seconds later, Penny swings onto the runway and we take to the skies again.

This whole takeoff procedure has become routine for the most part. There isn't much in the way of collisions or crashes anymore. All the weak sisters have been weeded out. Bombers take to the air and climb to join the formation without incident.

We are Tail End Charlie today. I like being the last plane in the group. I have a clear view all around. I have free range with my guns. Most guys don't like it, I do.

The formation starts pulling contrails as we climb out. I am surrounded by them. From my turret, it is a spectacular sight. They give the illusion of convergence in the distance. They are pretty, but dangerous. The bad thing is they obscure my field of vision. Everywhere I look white streaks fill the sky.

I could never see a Kraut in this. The contrails stop as the group breaks into a different temperature layer. The formation continues to climb in a crystal clear sky. Here come our escorts. P-38s, what a plane. They shepherd us into enemy territory.

Jesus, what is it with this FLAK? Cringing in my seat is my instinctive reaction every time. This anti-aircraft is the heaviest I have seen yet. CRUMPH, CRUMPH, the muffled explosions can be heard. If you can hear it, it is entirely too close. The FLAK goes off with a flash. Hot steel rockets across the sky. A black cloud of smoke marks where it detonates.

I put my knees together and lean forward. I scrunch my shoulders in trying to make myself as small as possible. There isn't any place to hide. The FLAK hammers away as we begin our attack.

I feel so naked every time we turn on the I.P. The formation flies straight and level into the target. Now is when we are most vulnerable to any form of attack. The way the FLAK is coming up, how can anybody aim at anything? The strict discipline of the bombardier always takes us over the target. Everybody in the group drops on the lead planes signal.

From my tail end perch, I get a perfect view of the strike. A blanket of bombs saturates the rail yard. The whole area is swept under. Everything is obscured by the smoke from the attack. We have pounded the target. As quick as it begins, it ends.

CRUMPH, CRUMPH, this turret will be my coffin. I know it. The formation wheels on the heading for home.

CRUMPH, CRUMPH, damn this FLAK. Nick starts his weaving between the brackets once again. We zig-zag on the tail end of the formation until we are out of the anti-aircraft gunners range.

We are not harrassed by enemy fighter. They didn't even come up. That's O.K. with me. The Lightnings didn't have any action today either. All they did was watch us fly through FLAK. The warm sun shines on my face as we cross the channel. It feels good to be alive. The P-38s fly with us under the brilliant sun. We are minute in a vast sky.

I make my way to the flight deck as we cross the English coast. Joe Craft waves me over. He tells me he thought he was hit pretty badly.

He points to a hole that the sun shines through next to the radio equipment. A piece of FLAK came through the fuselage and hit him in the face. It stung badly and he didn't know if it was a serious wound. He hurried to the flight deck to have Nick look him over. Nick told him, "No blood, you're O.K." The shrapnel impacted just off the corner of his eye. The result is a big purple welt. He is lucky. In the cold, it's hard to tell how severe your wounds are. The frigid temperature numbs everything.

Once over Old Buck, Nick brings Penny in. We roll past parked bombers that are being serviced as we taxi down the line. Our pilots pull Penny onto her hardstand. After the propellers come to rest, the ground crew chocks the wheels. A tired crew emerges from under the plane.

Pssssssssstt, Joe Craft's Mae West inflates. He's the lucky guy and he wins the prize. Hooting and laughter erupts as Joe starts to grow a yellow set of boobs. His smirk turns to laughter as the life preserver inflates around his neck.

A smoke is enjoyed as we get out of our flight gear. We recount the mission as we wait for the truck. At debriefing, all the interrogator's questions are answered. After that, it's off to the mess hall.

Once again, Charlie has something special for us. We take a slow walk to our hut on full stomachs. We have a day off tomorrow. A trip into Attleboro would be something to do. I put an entry in my diary and say my prayers before I drift off. I want to live.

#23; Alerted; May 22nd; Orleans, France: Airfield. The orderly wakes us up. Already? I feel like I just went to sleep. I roll out of bed and put my boots on. The Carter crew joins us as we walk to the mess hall. Breakfast is bread and jam with a cup of coffee to wash it down. Nobody wants to fly a six hour mission on a full stomach.

The crews that are flying today's mission assemble in the briefing building. Everybody carries on until we are called to attention. The officers tell us to sit down, then the briefing begins. We will strike Orleans, France. The airfield there will be bombed again. We are told we will wipe this target off the map. We will have a Mustang escort, Amen.

After the briefing, we grab our flight bags. Next stop is the parachute hanger. I grab what I believe is a good one. Guys hit the latrine one last time. A smoke is burned waiting for the truck.

By 2:30 A.M., we are at the plane getting ready in the darkness. Everybody prepares their stations as Nick and Luther go through the preflight checklist.

With a shout of clear, the starter begins to whine. It turns the propeller a few revolutions until the cylinders start to catch. With a cloud of white smoke, each mighty radial engine comes to life. All the engines are run up then brought to a smooth idle. Penny is buttoned up and we're off into the dim light of a new day.

The pins are pulled from the bombs as we cross the channel. I step over the turret well as I make my way aft. The first thing I do when I reach my station is unlock the turret. The guns are worked in the early morning sky.

The formation climbs through the rarefied air to cruising altitude. Our little friends shepherd us across the channel. Boy, we have a lot of escorts today. Nobody is getting near us. It would have been nice to have had them from the start.

Bomb groups that were formed early in the war had it rough. Some of these groups were flying as early as 1942. The 44th, 91st and the 93rd took beatings. Many men lost their lives. They were the guinea pigs. They pioneered the daylight bombing doctrine.

These guys wrote the book on tactics. They took the brunt of the German air defense. They developed the tactics we use now. These crews flew early model B-24s and B-17s. The armament wasn't as good as it is now. Enemy FLAK and fighters tore them to pieces. Losses were frightening and the daylight bombing doctrine was almost abandoned. After fighter escort was decided upon, the losses became tolerable.

Son-of-a-bitchin FLAK! There it is, out in the distance. Stay out there. I laugh to myself. This is insane. I have to be a lunatic to keep doing this. The Mustangs fly around it. Not us, we follow a flight path right through it.

We follow our preset course to the target. The formation turns on the Initial Point to start the bomb run. The moment the lead plane drops its bombs, the group rains high explosives on the airfield.

Penny lurches up free of her payload, as Leslie calls out, "Bombs away." Pure tonnage pulverizes the air base. Each salvo adds to the destruction. After the formation crosses over the target, we turn for home.

Fighters fly on our wing as we begin the return leg. They fly in finger four or echelon around the bombers. Not a single Kraut fighter comes up to do battle. There is not any FLAK either. We cross the channel unmolested.

We return to England bound for Old Buck. The Mustangs peel off for their own base. Our formation crosses the lush farmland of East Anglia on our way to Station #144. Penny waits her turn as we fly circuits over the base. Ten minutes later, Nick sets her down.

I feel pretty good as we emerge from the bomb bay. Maybe we will make it. There is no doubt the escorts keep the Krauts off our backs. I believe Nick's juking on the edge of the formation has saved us many times.

Major Stewart comes out to get the officers. He yells

out, "Hey, Black Fury," as he passes in his jeep. I smile and toss a crisp salute at the major. He smiles and gives me a wink as he pulls up to the plane. The officers gather around him. We wait for the truck.

Joe Craft hatches his .45 pistol scheme at debriefing. The story he tells the officer goes like this: "We had a bomb hang up on the rack. I was in the bomb bay trying to jar it free. I accidently hooked my pistol on the bomb rack as I was jimmying the bomb. When the bomb suddenly fell free, I lost my balance and the .45 was yanked out of its holster. The pistol now sits on the bottom of the English Channel. The debriefing officer tells him to go get issued another .45."

Laddy and I go with Joe and wait while he is issued a replacement side arm. With the first half of his scheme complete, we head to the mess hall. Joe calls Charlie over to the table as we sit down. With a grin on his face, Joe produces his old pistol. He tells Charlie, "Here you go." A smile appears across Charlie's face. He quickly tucks it away under his apron. He quietly thanks us before he goes back to his duties. We enjoy a nice meal before we go off to the shack.

I send my mom money in a letter. I tell her to get my little sisters some ice skates or something. I think of my girl in London, then Helen. Helen is my future. My girl in London is today. There may not be a future for me, but I am alive now. The path of this mission is traced on my map, I date it, and stow it away. Another entry is placed in my diary before I head to the showers. It will feel good to get this grime off of me.

#24; Alerted; May 25th; Troyes, France: Airfield. This will be another long one, seven hours. We are to expect FLAK and fighters, but we will have escorts. Once again, we hop on the Duce and a Half and ride out to the plane. I stand watch under the wings as Nick and Luther fire Penny up.

The sound of starting bombers carries across the fields. The 453rd begins to wake up. I wonder how it sounds to the locals when an airbase has all of its planes running. I wonder how it sounds when all the bases in East Anglia are up and running. It has to drown out everything across the countryside. There are quite a few bases only a few miles apart.

Penny takes her place in the line of bombers taxiing down the ramp. We slowly move forward until we reach the head of the strip. Nick wheels Penny onto the runway and guns the throttles. Penny careens down the strip. We are committed. There is not enough runway left to abort. We either take to the skies or crash and burn.

Penny leaps into the sky. Our bomber climbs out over the windmill that stands guard at the end of the runway. God only knows why nobody has crashed into it. You'd think that it would have been razed by now.

We climb until we are a little above the group. Nick then puts our bomber into a shallow dive and falls into place. We fly in a big circular pattern until the rest of the 453rd joins up. We follow "Wham Bam" to our place in the formation. The attack force is ready to start its journey to Troyes, France. The Lightnings join us as we cross the channel. They are our shepherds today.

It is time to get to my turret. The safety pins are pulled from the 500 pound bombs along the way. Once I position myself, the turret is unlocked and the guns are charged. When we climb over 10,000 feet, everybody goes on oxygen. I'm ready to go. It is a waiting game now, I wait to get killed.

CRUMPH, we enter a black cloud of FLAK. A dread feeling comes over me. I should have a nervous twitch or worse. The anti-aircraft explodes all around us. I don't think Nick's maneuvers are going to help. The formation stubbornly forges on. Nick reports a cloudbank ahead. I hope we get there before I get killed. Penny stands her ground as the FLAK reaches up to bring her down.

WHAM. The tail vibrates violently. What the hell is going on? Thoughts flash through my mind in an instant.

Am I still attached to the plane? Did Penny just get her tail blown off? Yes, I am still hooked to the plane. A look to my right, the tail looks good. A quick glance to the left reveals a huge hole in the rudder. An 88 mm. round has found its mark in Penny's tail.

Nick calls back, "Are you there Survilla?" I report, "Yes, but we got a big hole in the rudder." Nick can feel the vibration through his controls. He asks, "What's the situation?" I tell him, "Work the surfaces." Everything appears in working order, but a portion of the rudder is gone.

The air cannot travel over the damaged surface clean and it is causing the vertical stabilizer to wobble rapidly. This translates into a vibration that can be felt through the plane. The vibration could cause the rudder to break off. It feels like the tail is ready to let go at any moment. Even though Penny is stricken, she holds formation.

We turn on the I.P. over the cloudbank. Word filters back, the target is obscured. We have zero visibility. Set course for secondary target. The formation turns for Tarrenes, France. Powell plots our course and checks our fuel status. We are good to go.

An occasional FLAK burst comes up through the overcast. It isn't accurate, but it only takes one round to bring us down. I sit here waiting for Penny's tail to fall off. I just want to land. I want to get out of this plane. I wonder if I can get my parachute on if the tail snaps off. I set my chute right behind the turret.

The formation turns on the I.P. of the secondary target. The clouds open to expose the airfield below. The FLAK immediately targets us. The bomb bay doors are opened as we approach the release point. Leslie drops on the lead plane's mark.

"Bombs away," is called out as Penny rises relieved of her deadly cargo. Bombs rain down on the airfield. The following aircraft saturate the target area. The bomb bay doors are closed as the formation turns for home.

The FLAK continues to hound our crippled plane. Will we get hit again? Will the tail break off? How much time do

I have to get out of here if it does? Oh, God help me. I fear this will be my last mission. Help me, God. This FLAK will not stop. The group mercifully flies into the cover of another cloud- bank.

In the distance, P-38s tangle with the Me-109s they have intercepted. Two Lightnings chase a Tin Can as it scrambles to the deck. The three aircraft power dive recklessly, toward the ground. Before the P-38s can line up a shot, the German pilot flips open the canopy. He squats on his seat and springs out of the fighter. The pilotless aircraft plows into the ground. The exploding Me-109 showers wreckage across the deck. The dirty rat, bastard German floats to the ground unharmed. The P-38s drove that Hun right into the deck. That's a hell of a sight! The Lightnings zoom away victorious.

Penny continues to vibrate as we journey home. The crews of surrounding bombers curiously watch us. Is it that bad? Nick calls back on regular intervals for updates. The situation remains the same. Penny does hold formation easily. The problem is the vibration.

Laddy asks Nick if we can make it. Nick tells the crew, "Don't worry, Survilla is back there praying a Novena for us." Everybody laughs. The tension is relieved, but the vibration scares me. Penny's tail has to break off.

A P-38 pulls up alongside us. The pilot is obviously separated from his squadron. They are long gone. The Lightnings turned for home low on fuel after they tangled with the Germans. He joins the bomber formation off our wing. The pilot comes in on our frequency, "Escort me home big brother. I am out of ammo."

The Lightning flies off our wing as if he is escorting us. That's O.K. with me. It is a relief to have a fighter with us even if he is out of ammo. The pilot casually examines the hole in Penny's vibrating tail as we journey home. Once we cross the channel, the Lightning waggles its wings and it is gone.

The tail situation remains the same as we approach Old Buck. I take my crash landing position as Turwilliger shoots a red flare into the sky. The emergency personnel will be ready. Nick and Luther gently coax Penny in. Nick flares his Liberator out and carefully sets her down. He taxis our crippled bird to her hardstand. Relieved, the pilots shut her down.

Everybody hurries out of the plane to examine the damaged tail. Ooh, wee, it is about a three-foot hole with smaller holes peppering the edges. There are random shrapnel holes in the immediate area. The vertical and horizontal surfaces have damage, also.

I dig a few pieces of shrapnel out of Penny's tail with my knife. I'll keep these for souvenirs. The ground crew surveys the damage, then gets to work. The rudder will be replaced and all the damage repaired.

After we are debriefed, we head to the mess hall for a bite. Charlie made us some steaks, but there is no way I am eating. I am too wound up. The rest of the guys have no problem chowing down. After they finish, we head to the barracks. Our B-24 will be down a day or two.

I cannot relax as I lay on my bunk. I am scared. It always hits you after the mission. How many times can I beat the odds? Penny our dog lays on his blanket by the stove. I give his scruff a good rub. His tail slowly wags as he watches me. I pray hard until I fall asleep.

#25; Alerted; May 28th; Merseburg, Germany: Synthetic oil refinery. We are to strike a synthetic oil complex. We will be going through the Ruhr Valley. This will be yet another long one. We will have Mustangs as escorts. We have a smoke before we grab our flight bags. We wait for Hansen as he uses the latrine one last time.

We pull each other aboard the truck that takes us out to the bomber. Our ground crew is good; Penny is always ready to go. Nick gives us final instructions before he climbs up to the flight deck. Our pilots start the preflight checklist as we go about our preparations.

We boost our navigator, weighed down by maps, into Penny. After Powell arranges his station, he will go to the flight deck and wait for takeoff. Everybody climbs aboard before Nick fires the engines. I wait under Penny's wing watching for problems. After the engines are set at idle, I climb up to the flight deck.

Luther takes Penny up today. The brakes are slowly released before she is taxied out. We join the idling bombers at the end of the strip. When it's our turn, Luther brings our silver Liberator onto the runway. He pushes the throttles wide open and we are off. Penny climbs to join the circling formation. The Bunched armada turns for Germany. Our escorts join us before we cross the channel. The Mustangs will keep the Krauts at bay. Those rotten Me-110s don't have a chance to lob cannon shells at us when we have escorts.

I accept my fate as the formation flies into a curtain of FLAK. Once again, I cower in my turret as angry bursts go off around the plane. I wrap my Rosary tight around my hand praying for salvation. The bright blue sky is obscured with black puffs of destruction.

Just hit me and get it over with. BANG, OUCH! My head, what the hell! Before my mind could register what has happened, I am violently driven off my seat. My head smashes into the top of the turret. I lift my flak jacket to examine my seat. There is a jagged hole in it.

Holy smoke, I immediately know what happened. My God! I should be dead. A FLAK burst went off directly under Penny's tail. A piece of shrapnel traveled through the plane and my seat. It now sits lodged in my flak jacket. That piece of steel should have gone up my ass and through my guts. The flak jacket saved my life.

The near miss has me spooked. Nick asks if everything is O.K. He knows the burst was fatally close. Turwilliger comes back to see if I am alright. The turret responds to the controls and I tell him, "Yes." He pats my shoulder then returns to his gun. The gravity of the situation has me shaken.

My stomach knots as a B-24 in our box takes a hit. The wounded Liberator dips a wing before it starts its violent journey to the earth. Bombers in the lower element take evasive action to get out of the stricken B-24's path. The quick reaction of a pilot saves ten men's lives. The mortally wounded aircraft leaves a crazy trail of smoke as it flat spins from the formation. Momentum tosses six black specks that are men away from the dying Liberator. All of their parachutes open.

God damn this FLAK! God damn those dirty Krauts! Where's that target? I hope we bomb those Kraut bastards into the Stone Age. Where's a Tin Can? Come on, I'll blow your god damn head off. My anger quickly gives way to apprehension.

We turn on the Initial Point to attack the oil refinery. We make the run on the target oblivious to the FLAK. The group drops on the lead bomber's cue. Leslie reports, "Bombs away."

I watch with sinister satisfaction as bombs sweep across the refinery. Each successive group drops their bombs on the target. Thick black clouds of smoke obscure everything below. Huge crimson fireballs erupt through the boiling inferno. I curse the dirty Krauts as the formation turns for home.

The lunacy continues. The anti-aircraft is relentless. I don't want to get killed. I want to live. I am so close to finishing my tour.

A B-24 and an 88mm shell converge five miles above Germany. This Liberator starts to fall back. Smoke streams from the waist gunner's windows. There is a fire on board. It could be oxygen tanks or fuel.

The propellers pull the B-24 through the sky like nothing is wrong. The pilot steers his bomber away from the formation. Four black specks that are men fall free of the dying Liberator. It's a race against time for the rest of the crew to get out.

BLAM, the bomber explodes with a brilliant flash. The wings hang in the sky for a moment as the propellers continue to pull them through the air. After agonizing seconds, they fall away. Another Liberator is reduced to junk that showers from the sky. Six men die between heaven and earth.

There will be six more letters home to bring sorrow to six more families. Come on Nick, get us through this. The quicker we get out of this stuff, the safer we are. We emerge from this aerial gauntlet to see waiting Mustangs.

The Mustangs take up positions around us as they bring us out of Germany. We are assailed by another barrage of FLAK. The formation changes altitude several times in an attempt to confuse the anti-aircraft gunners. Once we free ourselves of this barrage, the formation races for home.

We return to England under a clear, blue sky. The group starts flying circuits over the base. Penny flies a racetrack pattern as we wait our turn to land. The crippled planes with the wounded are first. After a few more circuits, we come in. Luther brings Penny to her hardstand and shuts her down. I excitedly tell the guys how close it was for me as we emerge from the bomb bay.

What is this, blood? There is blood on my boot. I take my boot off to see my sock soaked with blood. There are tiny holes in my jumpsuit. The guys watch me with a curious concern.

I quickly strip down to my underwear. How bad am I hit? Blood oozes from wounds on my shin and inner thigh. Wow, shrapnel hit me and I didn't even know it. I couldn't feel anything in the cold. In all the excitement, I didn't even notice.

Nick tells me to go to the flight surgeon to get taken care of. I tell him O.K., but I don't. After debriefing, I go to the barracks and clean my wounds. I have three little pieces of Kraut steel in my left shin. I have one in my right thigh. The piece in my thigh doesn't look too deep. I can just barely make it out under the skin. My wounds are small; the shrapnel can stay there. I'll just clean them and put some bandages on them. Who needs the flight surgeon? Who needs a Purple Heart? I just want to finish my missions. I will not be grounded again.

That was a scary mission. Another one we sweated hard. It seems like the closer we get to finishing, the hairier the missions become. Mail brings news of my brother. He is O.K. in a P.O.W. camp. Look what he did. Now it's just my mom and sisters at home.

#26; Alerted; May 31st; Lumes, France: Marshalling Yards. We are told to expect FLAK and fighters. This could be a bad one or it could be a milk run. I am sick of playing this odds game. This could be my last mission. It could be, I'm dead. I could be a prisoner of war. It could be, I don't care anymore. We gather our gear and wait for the truck. We toss our stuff on and ride out to the god damn plane.

The feeling is fatalistic as we put our gear on. Looking at the guys, I can't believe it. Where did all the young faces go? It was only a few months ago we all met. Everybody looks tired and haggard. Wrinkles crease their faces.

Hansen and Leslie crack me up. They look like raccoons. Their faces are pale where their oxygen masks cover their skin. Their foreheads are pale where their flight caps cover their skin. They both carry a nice dark tan around their eyes.

So, this is what war does to you. I wonder what chronic health problems will materialize later in life. This is a nasty game we play. Come to think of it, our humor has grown dark and sinister also. To kill is no problem. Personally, I have no regrets.

Nick starts the engines that could carry me for my last ride. Maybe we will be god damn dead in four hours. We get in our fat, silver pig and roll off the hardstand. I stick my head out of the cockpit escape hatch to get a good look at the bombers taxiing down the ramp.

I must confess; it is impressive every time. It overwhelms the senses. Yellow-tipped propellers pull bombers down the flight line. The noise is deafening. The smell of fuel permeates the air.

Once we reach the end of the runway, it is time to button Penny up. Nick turns our bomber on the main strip and guns the throttles. With a roar of the engines, we take to the sky. Penny climbs to take her place in the formation.

We circle with the group until all the bombers fall into place. Our rally ship guides us to our groups place in the strike force. We climb out on our way to Lumes.

The pins are pulled on the bombs before I go to my station. Maybe they will go off. A shiver runs down my spine as I position myself in my turret. Let me sit here and freeze. Yes, I have to put my mask on. God help me, I should pass out and die or anything like that. Maybe I can tear more of my face off. I can't even shave for Christ sake. The flight surgeon says a few more days then I'll be healed up, what ever.

Our escorts pull up and take position around us. The formation pierces the cloud cover as we enter France. Not so bad, other planes can be seen through the broken clouds. CRUMPH, CRUMPH, goddamn this FLAK. I just sit here, in this turret, and wait to get killed. Does this madness ever end?

The anti-aircraft comes up but it isn't very accurate, until I get blown apart. The clouds do give a certain amount of protection from it. Brackets still pepper the sky anyway. The formation prepares to drive home the aerial assault. We follow the lead bomber to the I.P.

We fly straight and level. Yes, straight and level into a FLAK burst. I imagine Penny taking one on the chin like an upper cut from a boxer. The formation stays locked in its preset altitude. We maintain position as Penny shakes off the anti-aircraft bursts exploding around her.

Come on Leslie, let's hear, "Bombs away." This damn FLAK is getting a bead on us. What's the hold up? CRUMPH, that one was a little too close. Nick informs the crew that the target is obscured. Visibility is zero. We will continue to the secondary target.

The formation turns on the new heading. Nick starts his dance across the sky as brackets of FLAK reach up for us. We fly out of the barrage into the partly cloudy sky. A white blanket of clouds begins to spread out beneath us again. Moments later, the formation turns on the Initial Point of this secondary target. Once again, we fly straight and level.

Leslie announces, "Bomb bay doors opened." We wait for our bombardier's words. We hear nothing. Nick announces, "Mission scrubbed, the secondary target is socked in." Mother Nature spares the target today. We turn for home with a full bomb load. Black puffs appear sporadically as the FLAK gunners try to get another kill.

Here I am, somewhere over Paris getting shot at. How the hell did I wind up here? I swear jumping off the train in Luzerne was a million years ago. It all seems like a different life. It feels like that was someone else. At least the skies are clear of bandits.

The formation crosses out of France. Nick tells me to put the pins back in the bombs. I climb out of my turret to go forward. Oh no, what happened? One of the guys is down. I hurry to see what is wrong. His eyes are closed but he appears to be O.K. I give him a light kick that opens his eyes. He looks at me with a startled expression. I motion, "Are you alright?" He shakes his head, "Yes." "What's wrong?" I motion. He gives me a look that says nothing is wrong.

My anger instantly boils over. With another kick, I tell him, "Get up you son-of-a-bitch. Do you want to get us killed?" The offending crewmember pulls himself up and returns to his post.

I know the cold saps the energy out of a person, but we depend on each other. The incident begins and ends right there. Nothing is ever said.

Laddy spins in the ball turret as I step around the well into the bomb bay. I reinsert the pins into the bombs.

The bombs are the sole purpose of this plane. It's the sole purpose of any bomber, to carry the bombs. Nick and Luther's sole purpose is to fly the bombs to the target. Powell's sole purpose is to navigate the bombs to their destination. Leslie's sole purpose is to drop the bombs on target. For us gunners, our only purpose is to protect the bombs.

It is all about the bombs. Bombs destroy the enemy. We are expendable. The bombs are not. A bomb bay full of high explosives is more important than I am, god damn.

We follow our rally ship over Norfolk. The group starts circling over Old Buck. We fly a few circuits until we come in. We land faster than usual because we are heavy with bombs. Nick flares Penny out and we touch down. He quickly clears the strip so the next plane can come in. Our Liberator is parked and shut down.

A tired Crew 41 emerges from Penny's bomb bay. Pssssssst, Leslie spins around in an attempt to catch the culprit. It's too late. His Mae West inflates around his neck. Leslie puts his arms up in surrender then hangs his head in defeat. Everybody laughs and hoots.

The ordancemen pull up while we get out of our flight gear. They unload the bombs as we wait for the truck. They will be returned to the dump.

The Duce and a Half carries us down the flight line to debriefing. Oh well, this mission was a bust. We get good news after interrogation though. This mission will count. That makes four more to go, then I am done. I hope we make it. Thank God we are all safe.

We have some down time. Bad weather keeps the 453rd from flying. It is a rainy, ugly evening as Laddy, Joe Craft and I head into town. Our objective is the pub.

A staff car pulls alongside of us. Nick gets out and asks me where my rain gear is. He asks me if I like getting wet. "No sir," is my reply. Nick pushes his raincoat in my hand. He tells me to give it back when I return to the base.

We sit down to a dinner of fish and chips. The locals always come talk with us when we are around. They like hearing about Jerry getting his. We share stories of lethal encounters with the enemy. We always share a smoke with our local friends. We have a few drinks and chat for awhile. A conversation could go on for hours, it is fun.

We hitch a ride back to the base in due time. The M.P. once again gives a disapproving look. "Nice jacket," he comments as we walk through the gate. Yeah, nice jacket I think to myself.

I remember when all of us had "Lucky Penny" painted on them. We now have twenty-seven bombs and seven kills added to it. They are a status symbol. You can tell who the vets are by the number of bombs painted on their jackets. Names like Berlin, Gotha, Siracourt, Brunswick and Friedrichshafen adorn them. Some of the jackets have good paintings of naked women on them, too.

Vets, I am a vet? We have only been here five months. It feels like a lifetime. I have seen some things that will never go away. I know I will carry them with me until the day I die. We take a leisurely stroll to our Nissen hut. We load the stove with coal before we hit the rack. A vet, I laugh to myself as I doze off to sleep.

#27; Alerted; June 4th; Romorantin, France: Airfield. This will be a late mission. We are told to expect FLAK and always beware of fighters. They could appear anytime. Be aware of the possibility of night fighters also. After the briefing, we get our parachutes. I take one last stop at the latrine before we go out to the truck. We ride to the plane in the late morning sun.

The ground crew has just finished loading Penny's guns when we arrive. Nick does the walk around as Luther goes up to the flight deck. Once everybody prepares their stations, they come back out for a smoke. After a few minutes, we are told, "Everybody in." I standby under the wing as Nick starts the bomber up. Everything looks good, and I hop up on the catwalk. With a thumbs up, the bomb bay doors are closed

I get to watch the 453rd taxi out in the late morning sun. I open the escape hatch and take a seat on Penny's back. I watch a bomber takeoff every thirty seconds. A tap on the leg is the signal to get in. Nick turns on the runway then guns the throttles. We thunder down the strip into the early afternoon sky. Nick pilots Penny up to the circling B-24s. Once everybody is assembled, the formation turns for the enemy coast.

I climb into my turret as soon as we start crossing the channel. I strap on my mask and unlock the turret. After the intercom jack is plugged in, I charge the guns. The sky is empty of the enemy, but I'm ready.

The time is spent humoring myself reading the names of the surrounding bombers. There are names like Hoo-Jive and Silent Yokum. YUVADIT, there is a big painting of the middle finger on the side of that plane. Hah, hah, that's a good one. Lonesome Polecat, Vampin Vera, Male Call and Partial Payment are the names of a few others.

Some of the planes have close to thirty bombs painted on them. These are the vets. The vets, I laugh to myself again. The replacement crews fly in the middle of the formation. The German fighter pilots know by a plane's name who the veteran crews are.

The Germans see "Lucky Penny II" and they know the story. They know they got the plane, but not the crew. They know they must attack this part of the formation with caution.

As soon as we reach the French coast, the anti-aircraft starts. CRUMPH, CRUMPH, a black cloud erupts in front of us. CRUMPH, I hate this. We are almost done with our tour and we have to fly right into this stuff. Let me start my prayers, I want to live.

CRUMPH. I don't like when I can hear the FLAK going off. That means it is entirely to close. Penny is rocked and pitched, but there is nothing a person can do. I sit here helpless.

Joe Craft has a hard time hearing anything as he fights his electronic war on the radio. He deals with constant interference. The Krauts try to jam the radio waves with signals that leave weird screech tones in his earphones.

Long monotones, intermittent tones or warbling tones crowd his headset. The tones get louder as we approach radio beacons. He deals with constant background noise when messages are sent or received.

Joe has to watch out for false transmissions. They are weapons in the war of deception. The Krauts try to send up course corrections or recalls in an attempt to divert the bombers. If the ruse works, FLAK and fighters could be prepared, just waiting to knock us out of the sky. The raids are flown in radio silence to counteract this. Joe has his codes for the mission, and knows what's going on.

The FLAK continues to pelt the formation as it turns on the I.P. Locked in the run, we are at our most vulnerable. The formation forces its way through the man made cloud of destruction. Amazing, everybody is still here.

Leslie's voice comes through the headset, "Bomb bay doors opened." Moments later, Penny lurches as the bombs fall free. Leslie calls out, "Bombs away."

From my seat, I watch the strike. The smoke of the marker bomb arcs toward the airfield. It disappears in the distance. Moments later, the airfield erupts as tons of bombs violently smash it. The airfield is concealed under a pall of smoke. The strike looks good.

CRUMPH, CRUMPH, the FLAK intensifies as we turn for home. The formation flies into a cloudbank, not for cover, but because the weather is deteriorating. The report is a weather front is moving in over the French coast. Visibility is zero to the ground.

This is not good. It is getting dark and the skies are clouding up. Instead of FLAK, we can worry about crashing into each other. Darkness descends on the formation as it races west. The B-24s fade into shadowy figures in the waning light. We fly home, spread in a loose formation.

We cannot out run the night that falls upon us. The harsh glow of the exhaust tips are the only visible signs of an aircraft as darkness fades to black. Nick and Luther must trust their instruments. They can only hope everybody holds their position in the formation.

It is utterly spooky sitting in the blackness of this turret; I can barely see Penny's tail surfaces. All eyes strain, the whole crew is on edge. Everybody is ready to call out the moment they spot the shadowy figure of a Liberator drifting into Penny.

Powell confirms we are on course. If everybody continues to hold position, we should be O.K. Nick announces we are crossing over the channel. It all looks black to me. If we collide with somebody now, we will simply disappear. We will fall into the channel and sink. With the darkness and fog, we wouldn't have a chance.

There is no relief from the utter darkness as we approach the coast of England. It is pitch black, nothing can be seen. All pilots are informed they are on their own, use your best judgment.

Nick picks up the radio beacon of a Royal Air Force base near the Cliffs of Dover. He makes the decision to land there. It is too risky to attempt Old Buck. Joe Craft radios our base to inform them of our intentions.

We turn onto final approach at the R.A.F. base. The landing lights are useless; they cannot penetrate the fog. Our instruments say we are in the flight path. Nick rides the radio beam to the strip. At the last moment, runway lights penetrate the fog. With a crow hop, we touch down. Our pilots keep Penny between the lights as we coast to the end of the strip. That was scary.

Our B-24 idles at the end of the runway waiting for instructions. We are told the approaching jeep will take us to our parking spot. Nick keeps the jeep in the landing lights as we follow it to our temporary hardstand. Relieved, we wait for our pilots to shut Penny down. After the propellers come to a stop, we emerge from under her.

It feels good to be on solid ground. We take our flight gear off and stow it in the plane. It is late; my watch reads 11:00 P.M. We are stuck at a British base, but we are alive. The whole crew sweated this out like you wouldn't believe. Nick and Luther are good pilots.

A truck comes out to pick us up. The driver shouts out, "Hi, Yanks, are you hungry?" We climb aboard and it takes us to the mess hall. We are met by the British equivalent of our W.A.C.'s. What nice girls. They treat us well. The food truly is good. After we finish, we are directed to a barracks to spend the night. The whole crew sleeps together. The beds are great, they are better than ours. We have no problem dozing off in such comfortable racks.

An orderly awakens us at dawn. I put on my boots, then join the rest of the crew outside. We proceed to the mess hall with Nick leading the way. Everybody there is cordial. We get a friendly greeting or a smile as we sit down to breakfast. The base commander comes to pay us a visit. He is a gentleman. He asks us if we are enjoying our accommodations. We answer "Yes sir" in the proper military fashion.

He asks Nick if he would like to take a ride in a Mosquito. He informs Nick, "Your plane is being serviced and you have some time." This opportunity cannot be past up. We go out to the plane to watch.

A lone B-24 sits crashed off the end of the runway. The British ground crew tells us, "That B-24 came in last night, just before you." Powell grabs his camera and snaps a picture of it.

Our attention is turned to the sound of a plane taking off from the opposite end of the runway. An R.A.F. Mosquito streaks past, and gracefully climbs into the morning sky. Nick is getting a real treat. The British call the Mosquito, the Wooden Wonder. It is a twin-engine fighter / bomber that is mainly built of wood. The Mosquito is a fast and agile aircraft. It is used for anything from bombing to path finding. It is also used for reconnaissance and special operations.

We admire the plane's ability as it dances across the sky. The base commander puts the Mosquito through its paces. He does a couple rolls then climbs into big graceful loops. He then screams down the runway at zero altitude, "Boy, that's a good-looking plane!"

After they are finished, Nick is given a ride out to Penny by our host. He excitedly tells us about his flight. The base commander is given a tour of Penny in return. Nick takes the British Officer to the flight deck as Luther starts running down the checklist.

After a while, the base C.O. emerges from the bomber smiling. Leslie offers him a smoke. The commander is gracious enough to have a cigarette and chat with us. We thank him for his hospitality. He replies, "Your welcome, Yanks." We salute our host and climb aboard our B-24.

Penny's engines stumble and cough to life with puffs of

white smoke. The engines are run up and we taxi out. The base commander stays on the flight line to see us off. Nick puts the throttles forward and we take to the air. We climb over the crashed B-24 into the morning sky.

It is a short hop to Old Buck. With a squeal of the tires, Nick brings us home. We emerge from under Penny after a harrowing night. Our ground crew is happy to see us. We tell them about our bad weather detour over a smoke. The truck arrives to carry us to debriefing. We answer all the questions we are asked and head to our shack.

We will stay on the base. We will be flying again tomorrow. I think I'll write some letters or square away my area. Maybe take the dog for a walk. I have to get to bed early though. Who knows what tomorrow brings. I write an entry in my diary, then trace the path of this mission on my map. I thank God for bringing us home safe.

#28; Alerted; June 5th; Normandy, France: Invasion Points. The rumor is, be ready for tomorrow. The invasion may be on. Nobody can sleep. It sounds like it is going to happen this time. At 11:00 P.M.,George Neamy hurries into the shack to tell us the base is under lockdown.

The M.P.s have been sent out to bring back aircrews that are out with passes. An orderly informs us we will be briefed shortly. This must be the Big Show. We'll see, we were told to stand down before.

Everybody hurries to the briefing. Crews that got the word straggle in as we receive instructions. There will be multiple sorties today. We listen to the operations officers intently. Our attacks will be tactical. We will be bombing the coastal area of Normandy, France. We will be dropping bombs at 6:12 A.M. on the invasion points. This will be 18 minutes before our troops hit the beaches. This is the Big Show. The invasion of Europe is on.

We will be with the first group to takeoff at 3:00 A.M. The briefing is discussed in animated tones as we go to the parachute hanger. We grab our chutes and wait for the truck to carry us out to Penny.

There is activity everywhere; this is going to be some kind of a day. We expect that the Krauts will throw everything at us. There is no doubt the fighter attacks will be vicious. The FLAK should be like nothing I've ever seen before. I am prepared for the worst. My pistol is ready if I have to bail out. Guns and equipment are checked many times over.

Nick and Luther start the preflight checklist as we nervously burn a smoke. Is this where my life's journey ends? Is this my fate? The odds do not look very good.

Everybody climbs into Penny. With a shout of clear on two, the propeller starts to turn. Penny slowly comes to life. Our ground crew watches with apprehension as Nick brings the engines to an idle. The wheel chocks are pulled and we are given the thumbs up. The brakes are released, and we taxi off the hardstand. We are cheered on as we rollout.

All of the ground crews watch the planes taxi down the flight line. Any base personnel that can, have gathered to watch. You can feel it in the air. It is exciting, and I swallow hard at the same time. I clutch my Rosary tight.

Nick swings our Liberator onto the runway without losing momentum. He immediately guns the throttles. Huge flames leap from the exhaust as Penny thunders down the strip. The landing lights fade in the night as Penny jumps into the predawn sky. Our B-24 climbs to take her place in the circling formation. We cross the channel in the darkness of an ominous new day.

The dimly lit, predawn sky reveals shadowy aircraft everywhere. All the fighters and medium bombers, in theater, are now wearing multiple white and black stripes. They wrap around the wings and fuselages of all the aircraft. High command has ordered this for the invasion. These stripes have been painted on for easy identification. You cannot miss them; they look gaudy as all hell.

We leave a crowded sky behind as we fly to the target. The safety pins are pulled on the bombs before I go to my station. Victor and Turwilliger get a pat on the shoulder in passing. We may die before the morning is over. Once on my seat, I charge the guns, they are ready. The turret is put through its paces. Everything is set.

This is it, the invasion. We will finally have troops on the ground in Hitler's Fortress Europe. I pray we are successful in doing our part. We will soften German positions right before our troops assault the beaches.

The formation flies into the gloomy morning sky. The invasion comes into view below. I crane my neck to get a look. There are ships of all shapes and sizes assembled here. It is awe-inspiring. It appears there are ships all the way back to England. It looks like you could walk across the channel on them.

The Navy shells the beaches. The cruisers and destroyers sail in a pattern that resembles half of a football. On the straight leg of the pattern, the ships bombard the beach. When a ship is done traversing the straight length of the pattern, it turns on the arc of it to cool its guns. The warships follow this pattern over and over as they shell the beaches. German bunkers and fortifications are repeatedly pounded by the naval bombardment.

The menacing battleships lurk further back. They duel with the coastal batteries. When they fire their sixteen-inch guns, the sea ripples around them. Smoke and fire belch from the barrels of these battlewagons. Huge shells are rocketed at the beach. These rounds obliterate whatever they strike. The battleships raise their massive guns skyward to hit inland targets. The Normandy coast is dotted with the explosions of the naval onslaught.

The troop transports lay back. The landing craft pull alongside these ships. Soldiers climb down cargo nets into them. The landing craft then circle next to the ships in a holding pattern. Their circuits resemble four leaf clovers. They wait for the command to assault the beach.

Everybody in Penny takes it in. Incredible, how can the Krauts resist the sheer weight of this massive assault!

Fighters patrol the coast. The Luftwaffe would be insane to come up and fight today. No doubt, this is the Big Show. What if we fail? How long will the war go on?

How many more missions will I have to fly? Will I live? Will we win the war? Oh God, grant us victory.

The formation turns on the I.P. It doesn't even look like we're over the beaches from up here. At 6:12 A.M., Leslie calls out, "Bombs away." It is exactly 18 minutes before the invasion starts.

Leslie informs us that the formation purposely released ten seconds late. We dropped our bombs a little further inland for fear of hitting our guys. The troops may not have assaulted the beaches yet, but there are frogmen and pathfinders that could be hit in the strike.

We turn for Old Buck as the naval bombardment lifts. The landing crafts come out of their holding patterns and start toward the shore. They fall into line abreast as they run in on the beaches. Geysers of water appear around them as they launch the assault. The troops are going in. "Get those Hun bastards!" I silently pray for them.

No FLAK and there sure aren't any fighters. A Kraut would have to be crazy to lock horns now. Just about every Allied plane is up here. We must observe assigned altitudes to avoid collisions. I can't help thinking about the invasion as I peer into a dreary, gray sky. What a sight! The Krauts must feel like the world is falling on them.

Penny arrives over Old Buck under an overcast sky. We fly a holding pattern until it is our turn to land. Nick tweaks the rudder as he brings Penny in. The kids are at the fence waving like mad, they have heard the news. The invasion of Europe has begun. Nick brings Penny off the runway and taxis to our hardstand.

There are excited tones in our conversation as we come out from under Penny. Our ground crew is eager to hear what we have seen. The mission is described to them over a cigarette.

The debriefing officers come out to the plane today. The ground crew gathers around. They listen intently as we are interrogated. The guys strain to hear every detail. They have done their part and are eager to hear the news of the invasion.

Powell asks a passing member of another ground crew

to take a picture of the guys. Carl gives his camera to the enlisted man. He steps back and snaps a photo of the crew being debriefed.

We are ordered to stay with the plane. All crews are ordered to stay with their aircraft. Nobody leaves the hardstands. The ground crews stay with their planes also. The kitchen staff brings sandwiches out to us; they want to know everything too. We take the time to answer all their questions.

We wolf down our food as the ground crew prepares Penny for another mission. The ordnance men pull up to load our bomber. They are excited like everybody else. We answer all their questions as well. They write messages to Hitler on the bombs before they are hung in the plane.

The consensus is the invasion will succeed. We sprawl out under Penny's wing as the officers of Crew 41 are briefed. After Nick receives his orders, he gathers us around.

#29; Alerted; June 6th; Normandy, France: Invasion Points. Nick briefs us next to the plane. This is our second mission of the day. This will be another tactical raid. We will be part of a five-bomber strike. We are going to bomb some highway. We are to stop German reinforcements that are trying to get to the coastal towns.

Nick and Luther bring "Lucky Penny II" to life. The engines are run up, then set to idle. Everything looks good. The chocks are pulled and the brakes released.

The ground crew cheers us on as we rollout. This is their plane, also. They are just as much a part of this and they take great pride in what they do.

Penny carries us down the runway, off into the afternoon sky. Our five-plane formation climbs into the overcast. I hate this, everybody strains searching for the tell tale shadow of another B-24. I shrink at the thought of Penny colliding with another plane. I imagine the tangled mess of two bombers crashing to the ground. We climb to

15,000 feet before we suddenly break out into a bright, clear sky. It is always sunny above the clouds.

I put my sunglasses on then search the horizon. All is clear. The formation crosses the channel above a white blanket of clouds. I will get to see how the invasion is progressing on the return leg. We cross over the invasion points unopposed. No FLAK or enemy fighters to be seen, only ours.

As we descend through the clouds, P-38s work out below. I watch them demolish a German convoy. Caught in the open is no place to be. The P-38s come straight down the road at zero altitude. The Krauts abandon their vehicles diving to the sides of the road in desperation. Bodies are tossed in the air as the Lightnings spit death out of their noses. The P-38s leave so much burning junk in their wake. They prowl the skies looking for another opportunity to strike.

The burning convoy disappears in the distance as we approach the target. We drop to the assigned altitude as we run in on the highway. We fly straight and level until Penny lurches upward. At the same moment, Leslie reports, "Bombs away." The formation turns for home. I get to see our handy work from my turret.

500 pound bombs rain on the highway. They penetrate the road surface before the delayed fuses set them off. The bombs devastate the road. Huge sections are pulverized. Vehicles that happen to be there pay the price. Tanks and trucks are tossed about like a child's toys. Some simply disappear in a direct hit.

We have made this section of road useless. The wreckage will have to be cleared before the road can be rebuilt. Our orders were to destroy this part of the highway. It looks destroyed to me. The shattered target shrinks in the distance as we head for home.

Our return leg takes us over the invasion points. I have a panoramic view from the best seat in the house. The invasion unfolds in front of me. There is a monumental struggle below. The magnitude of it assails the senses. On one section of the beach, the surf is red. The blood stained water stretches like a thin, red ribbon along the shoreline.

The channel is full of ships, but there is no movement towards the shore. There are landing craft burning in the water. There are men huddled against the seawall. It looks like they are pinned down by the Krauts on the high ground. Broken bodies lay in the surf and on the beach. Burning tanks and equipment are strewn about.

Cruisers and destroyers are dangerously close to the shore. They look like they will run aground. Their guns fire like mad. They blast German fortifications point blank. The bluffs are being pounded by the naval guns. It doesn't look good.

Other sections of beach are teaming with activity. Huge landing craft discharge vehicles and supplies. There are barrage balloons tethered over these ships.

These barrage balloons look like little blimps. They are raised to deter attacking aircraft. They suspend thick cables that are designed to mortally damage an aircraft on impact.

It looks like we have captured some of the coastal towns. Convoys of men and equipment move inland. Will we be driven back into the sea? I don't know. I wish I had a camera.

Our little formation continues its journey home. A scan of the sky reveals only allied aircraft. The black and white Invasion Stripes they carry cannot be missed.

We fly into another cold front. What a mess. I can't see a thing and it's starting to get dark. We have to stay alert. We are not home free yet. A collision would be a hell of a way to go.

The enemy could be anywhere. Darkness is a night fighter's friend. The British know about German night fighters. Some of those Limey bomber crews never saw it coming. They found out a Kraut was there when bullets started ripping their plane apart. Eyes are strained searching for the glow of an aircraft's exhaust. I search for the silhouette of an airplane against a darkening sky.

The weather deteriorates as we approach England. The overcast is to the ground. Once again, we have zero visibility. It's pretty much every man for himself. Nick and Luther put their trust in Penny's instruments once more.

Powell announces we are over East Anglia. Penny picks up Old Buck's radio beacon. Nick cautiously descends over the base. The altimeter tells the story. My instincts tell me we are close to the ground. Here's another way to go, fly into a house or just hit the ground. At about 100 feet, we break out of the dense overcast into a foggy mist. We ride the radio beacon on final approach.

All eyes peer into the darkness. We don't need another B-24 coming down on top of us. We don't need a bomber flying a different course slamming into the plane. I could think of a hundred different ways to die. Nick cautiously brings Penny in. The landing lights finally penetrate the gloom as we touch the runway.

The bomb bay doors are opened as we taxi to the hardstand. After Penny is shut down, we emerge from under her, tired but excited. Our ground crew is happy to see us. We tell them the stirring sights we have witnessed on this day. They want to hear more. They visualize the things we tell them. Some shake their heads in disbelief.

After I get out of my gear, I sink to the ground drained. It feels good to stretch my legs. I have been awake for just about forty-eight hours and I am exhausted.

The truck comes and takes us to debriefing. We don't have to wait in line. This was just a five-plane mission. We answer all the questions we are asked, then make our way to the mess hall.

The haggard faces of other aircrews turn our way as we settle at a table. We give each other nods of acknowledgement. The kitchen staff comes out to the tables to ask about the invasion. They too want to know everything.

There is an air of excitement at this midnight hour. Could this be the beginning of the end? Could this invasion mark the turning point of the war? It was a hell of a sight.

The worn out men of Crew 41 make their way to the barracks. What a day or should I say, what a two days. I fall into my bunk worn out, but the question still remains, will the Krauts throw the invasion back into the sea? I don't think so. I saw troops and equipment moving inland. It's been a remarkable day. It feels like I have been here for a thousand years. Hey! I have one more mission to go. The day's events fade into the haze of slumber.

(Note: June 6th, 1944 will be known as D-Day. The 453rd flew four missions on D-Day. "Lucky Penny" flew two.)

Morning brings a break. We are not flying today. Yesterday's events are the topic of discussion. We share our experiences with the Carter crew. Everybody has their own little piece of the invasion ingrained in their memory.

The talk of the Big Show is everywhere. The 453rd was ordered to bomb some coastal town with a historic cathedral in it. The word is we flattened the town and left the cathedral standing. Every crew has a different story. It is exciting! Everybody wants to know about it. Everyone from the doctors to the M.P.s want to hear what happened.

The people of England know the invasion has taken place. The folks back home know. The world knows. Hitler's Fortress Europe has been breached. Word of it is all over the radio and newspapers. The Allied forces have landed in Normandy, France.

This is evidently the biggest invasion there ever was. The situation at a beach called Omaha was pretty bad, but our boys broke out. Atlantic Wall, my ass. Rommel blew it in North Africa and he blew it in Normandy.

It isn't just the Air Corps anymore. At last, there are troops on the ground on the Western Front. Maybe we can finally step on Hitler's throat.

All I know is I fly tomorrow, and it is my last mission. Penny has got to carry us one more time. I want to live. I do not want to die.

#30; Alerted; June 8th; Flers, France: Invasion Points. We are told to expect FLAK and always be on the look out for fighters. We will have P-47s escorting us. We are going to bomb some Kraut strong points. These are areas where the Germans are putting up a stiff defense. They are stalling the breakout of the invasion. We grab our flight bags, then wait for the truck. This mission shouldn't be too bad. We will see.

We ride to Penny for the last time. We meet our ground crew in the predawn darkness. They wish us luck as we prepare for the mission. Nick and Luther climb up to the flight deck.

The pilots start the litany, generators off, main line and battery selectors on. Gyros uncaged, cowl flaps opened. The crew climbs aboard Penny. She is ready to go. Come on baby, one more time. I stand under the wing of our B-24 waiting for the engines to start. Luther hangs his head out the window and yells, "Clear on three."

The starter cranks the propeller a few times until the cylinders start to catch. This process is repeated three more times until Penny sits on her hardstand idling. Everything looks good. I climb aboard and the bomb bay doors are closed behind me.

Everybody waits in takeoff positions. Nick pulls Penny out into the orderly succession of bombers taxiing down the ramp. I wonder how many replacement crews we have flying with us today? I see new faces all the time.

Once again, Nick turns our bomber onto the runway. As soon as we are straight, he pushes the throttles wide open. Penny springs to life. She bolts down the runway, and jumps into the sky. We fly a holding pattern until the rest of the bombers form up.

The pins are pulled from the bombs on my way to the tail. As I pass through the rear bulkhead, I watch Laddy prepare to get into his turret. Turwilliger and Victor always help him.

Laddy flips the handle and lifts the hatch up. He positions his body and hangs his legs in the ball. With a wink, he slides in. Once Laddy is set, Turwilliger closes the hatch. He looks in on Laddy through the little observation window. Laddy gives the O.K. signal and Jim slaps the hatch twice. Laddy is ready to go.

The turret is lowered out of the well. Once Laddy is hanging in the breeze, he tests the controls. The turret looks like some monstrous eyeball as it spins around in the sky. God bless Laddy, he is a good guy. The formation flies to the target over the invasion points.

It is still a spectacular sight below. There is every conceivable ship on the water. Men and equipment stream from prebuilt docks that were floated across the channel. An artificial jetty sits out in the channel also. It too was floated over from England. The jetty protects the docks from the English Channel's currents. That is a feat in itself.

CRUMPH, CRUMPH, I can't believe we are being targeted. It is sporadic, but all it takes is one shot. I cringe on my seat, defenseless. Nick starts sliding in and out in the midst of intermittent bursts. Nothing has changed. The bombers boldly plow ahead. I can't get hit now. All I can do is sit here and sweat it out.

We begin our run on the target. Come on Penny, one more time, come on baby doll. Penny lurches upward as Leslie calls out, "Bombs away." Bombs rain on the enemy. The men and equipment disappear in violent explosions that alter the landscape. Napalm leaves fiery paths of destruction across the ground. Well, there is no hiding from 500 pound bombs or napalm.

The FLAK continues to hound us as we wheel onto the return leg. This is maddening; we better not get hit. I better not get killed now. As we cross over the beaches, they are beehives of activity. There is no throwing this invasion back into the sea. We are here to stay. Marauding Thunderbolts join us as we cross the channel for home.

I can't believe it. We made it. Thanks to God. No more sweating it out. No more FLAK, I hate that FLAK. No more just sitting here cringing in a turret. No more dueling with fighters. No more head on passes. No more flying in bad weather. No more tempting fate. No more praying myself to sleep.

This is anything but romantic. What a bunch of crazy, foolish, dumb asses we are. All we have to do is get Penny home. A search of the horizon reveals an empty sky. All is clear as we cross the channel.

Penny carries us across the English coast for the last time. After locking the turret, I make my way to the flight deck. I shake hands with Turwilliger and Victor as I go forward. Laddy gives me a pat on the shoulder in passing. Joe, Carl and Leslie greet me on the flight deck. Hanson reaches down from his turret to shake hands. I get between Nick and Luther. A quick shake of hands marks the end of flirting with death. We have beaten the odds. Crew 41 has survived.

The group approaches Old Buckenham. We begin to circle the base that I have been flying out of for the last six months. We fly circuits over the Norfolk countryside on a warm summer's day. The flaps are set and Luther lowers the landing gear. Nick brings Penny in on final approach. Hey, there aren't any kids to cheer us on at the fence. With a squeal of the tires, we are home. We taxi down the ramp to our hardstand for the last time. When the propellers stop, we emerge from under our girl.

This is it. I don't have to fly anymore. Everybody acts salty like we knew we would make it all along. The ground crew shares our victory with us. They swagger about the plane that they maintained. Yes, it is their planes, Penny I and II, that carried us through thirty missions.

Congratulations are exchanged with the ground crew. We walk around our B-24 with admiration. She has brought us back time after time. A cigarette has never tasted so good as we get out of our flight gear.

The truck carries us to debriefing. The other crews congratulate us as we wait in line to be interviewed. They know thirty missions is the magic number. They also know there is a possibility we can fly more. Nonetheless, there is hope in their eyes. We are proof it can be done.

The interrogators ask us what we saw up there. They give each of us a shot of rum and tell us to beat it. We go to the mess hall for a bite. We kick back reveling in our survival. The angel of death does not ride with us anymore. We talk about what we will do when we get back home. We make plans for tonight's celebration. Nick comes to join us at the table. He tells us straight out, "Go get some sleep. We are not finished." …"What?"

Dawn brings a new day, but we are not flying. The Grim Reaper has spared us at least one more time. We mope around the barracks in disgust.

Yes, the barracks. I wonder how guys feel that come back to an empty cot. How does a man feel when he gathers up the personal effects of a dead crewmate? Usually an orderly will do it. Superstition keeps people from doing certain things.

What was their friend's manner of death? Was it quick? Was there a call on the intercom only to be answered with silence or static? Did the crew hear a man's last words?

What sights greeted them when they went to check on a brother in arms? Was the wind whipping through a hollow space where a turret used to be? Were they accosted by a headless torso squeezing the controls tight with blood frozen to the plexiglas?

Did they find a friend with his life draining out of him? Did they look into an ashen face? Did they listen to him cry as he told them he didn't want to die?

Did they watch a mate contort in pain from an unseen, ghastly injury that drove him to horrific screams? Screams that send chills down the spine. All along his comforters hoping he would quickly die, so they wouldn't have to listen to the unnerving sounds. Did they hold a mortally wounded friend's hand waiting for death to relieve him of his agonizing hell? It is a hell of a thing, young men comforting each other as they die.

The more empty racks there are, the sadder the story is. What about a whole plane lost? The remaining crew gets to look at the beds of the crew they bunked with and ponder their own fate. How does a new crew come into a barracks with a seasoned one? How do you replace the bunks of friends?

How does a replacement crew introduce their selves to

a veteran crew? What about an empty barracks? Two crews lost. That must be spooky. A new crew has to believe they are jinxed as they move into the hut.

We are lucky. The Carter crew has survived along with us. I don't know about making it now. We should be done. Will our luck run out? What will be the fate of Crew 41, what is mine?

#31; Alerted; June 10th; Boulogne, France: Highways. We are awakened in the early morning hours once again. I contemplate my fate as I put my boots on. This is bullshit and I should be done. I sit on the edge of my bunk waiting for the guys to get ready. We step into the morning darkness of another day. We wait in line outside the mess hall. I really hate this. I dread the thought of going up again.

We are the squadron's guinea pigs now. Everybody knows we completed our missions. Can a crew make it after they complete their tour? We eat a light breakfast and go to the briefing.

At the briefing, we are told this will be another tactical strike. We will be bombing highways to block German reinforcements. We will be just outside of Paris, France. I don't like this. I don't like playing with my life again.

The truck takes us out to Penny. There she is. I do not want to get in that silver coffin. There isn't any false bravado as we gear up. There isn't anyone to fool. We know each other too well. We are scared and we don't want to do this. Nobody wants to fly this mission but it is our job.

The mood is subdued. We nervously burn cigarettes under Penny's wing as Nick and Luther start the preflight checklist. We try to be fatalistic about all of it, but we should be finished.

The guys grudgingly climb into the bomber and prepare their positions. The propellers start turning as Penny is awakened from her slumber. Nick slowly runs the engines up. All the gauges check out normal. The throttles are set at idle and Luther releases the brakes. The crew chief cannot be heard as he yells out, "Good luck!" He sends us on our way with a thumbs up.

We join the other bombers taxiing down the ramp. We wait at the end of the runway for our turn. We watch the B-24s methodically take off. Nick wheels Penny on the runway and guns the throttles. Our overloaded bomber thunders down the strip once again. At 130 miles per hour, he nudges the yoke. Penny leaves the ground beneath her. We are off to fight once more. We fly a holding pattern until the rest of the group forms up.

Penny falls into her customary position on the edge of the element. I unlock the turret and put my oxygen mask on. A quick search reveals an empty sky. I curse Hitler as the formation starts to pull contrails. They are pretty and all that, but I can't see a thing. It is hard to make out what is going on. The unmistakable silhouettes of P-38s appear above the bombers. They will be escorting us today.

It is no longer the enemy coast in some areas. The invasion has made advances inland. There are now towns occupied by us along the French coast. There are places we can safely bail out now. At the very least, we can work our way to friendly lines.

God help an aircrew that is shot down over Germany now. It has to be worse than ever. It's best to just let yourself get captured by the army. You do not want the civilians to get their hands on you.

CRUMPH, CRUMPH, panic wells up inside of me. I would like to believe I am used to this in some maniacal way, but in reality, I can't stand it. Nick zig-zags on the edge of the formation. It still works. A bracket goes off where we would have been. This deadly game is a matter of timing. If the gunners throw up some FLAK at the right moment, we are done.

The formation flies to the northeast of Paris. The city spreads out below. There's the tower. What the hell is the name of it? I can't think of it for the life of me.

We turn on the Initial Point. Once again, we fly straight

and level to the target. Penny's belly opens up in anticipation of delivering her deadly payload. Moments later, our Liberator lurches up as Leslie reports, "Bombs away." We have done our job so let's get the hell out of here.

Our handy work comes into view from my balcony seat. The bombed section of road is obscured by smoke. Well, we hit the highway. There is no doubt about that. I wonder how long it will take the Krauts to rebuild it. Who cares, get us home Nick.

The FLAK gunners double their efforts to bring a bomber down. Why doesn't our escort go down and shoot the shit out of those FLAK Carts? CRUMPH, oh Lord can we make it? Victor and Turwilliger stand at their guns like tourists. What else can they do? What a sight the two of them are. Flak jackets, helmets, oxygen masks make them look like they are from another planet.

A lot of good a flak jacket did for that blond haired waist gunner I occasionally talked to in the mess hall. I heard what happened to him. A 20 mm. round out of a Me-109 blew him in half. He came back all right, in two pieces. I really shouldn't talk. If it wasn't for my flak jacket, I would be dead.

The formation wheels for home. The planes on the inside of the turn throttle down. This is done to keep the strike force together through the maneuver. No losses yet, let's keep it that way. There isn't a Kraut to be seen as we journey home.

A formation of Thunderbolts prowls the skies below us. The invasion-striped planes are on the attack. They stick out like sore thumbs at any altitude. They are looking to blast anything that moves. No convoy, tank, or locomotive is safe.

The fighter pilots know all the Kraut's tricks. They shoot up haystacks that have FLAK guns hidden in them. They blast locomotives, houses and barns. The fighters hammer anything that could conceal German troops. Some of the targets strafed result in huge explosions.

The Lightnings escort us home. We fly over the fields

of East Anglia. Farmers look up as the shadows of passing bombers momentarily block out the sun. We get into a racetrack pattern over Station #144. Our circuits take us near the neighboring bases. The 389th, 455th, 452nd and the 96th Bomb Groups surround us. I hope this is the last time I look down on them.

There's those B-17s. They get all the credit. I don't know why. There are more Liberators in service. The B-24 carries twice the bomb load, flies faster and has a lot more range. That tells me that the B-24 is a better plane. It is true; the B-17 can take more punishment. Well, I hope the hell so, it is slower and it's over the target longer. It really doesn't matter, we all die the same. Death plays no favorites. As long as Penny gets us through this, there is no doubt that she is the best plane ever built.

After fifteen minutes, Penny is brought in; our co-pilot has the honor of landing her. With a squeal of rubber, we touch down. Luther brings our Liberator to the hardstand and shuts her down. Penny has carried us home again.

The ground crew greets us with smiles. We recap the mission with them over a smoke. Major Stewart arrives in his jeep and the officers pile in. The truck comes and carries us down the flight line to the debriefing.

After waiting for ten minutes, I answer all the questions the interrogator asks me. We wait on each other before we go to the mess hall. "I thought you guys were done?" Charlie asks, as he plops food on our trays. The meal we are served is good, but it does not sit well with us. We should be done.

We go to our barracks disgusted and angry. I trace today's mission on my map. It is dated and put away. I put yet another entry in the diary. After I page through it, it is stowed away. It is hard to believe we have flown thirty-one missions. I thank God for letting me live as I fall asleep.

#32; Alerted; June 11th; Cormeilles, France: Airfield. We will be striking an airfield today. Expect FLAK and be aware of fighters. A raid earlier today to LePort Boulet, France, was turned back due to weather. We will attack this new target instead. We are going back to doing what we do best, strategic bombing.

I've never noticed the new faces sitting around me. The replacement crews look to us vets. They pay attention to what we do. We act salty when we know we are being watched. I don't know anybody new and I don't want to.

We truck out to the plane. Can Penny do it again? The eleventh crew member joins us as we prepare for the raid. The fear of dying always gnaws at the back of my mind. Will it be today? I hope this mission is a milk run.

The ground crew has Penny ready as always. Nick and Luther run down the preflight checklist. They could probably do it with their eyes closed by now. With the yell of "Clear," the engines cough to life. Each one is run up before it is set at idle. There aren't any obvious problems, everything looks good. I give the O.K. signal when I climb aboard.

Nick rolls our B-24 off the hardstand. Things have become second nature. Our pilots know how to get the most out of her. Penny is taxied out to the ramp without a thought. We wait our turn as bombers bound down the runway. Our pilot keeps the forward momentum going as we swings onto the strip. He guns the throttles and Penny leaps into the air.

Our bomb laden B-24 climbs over the windmill once more. We are off to tempt fate again. After the group forms up, we turn for France. I can't believe I am flying again. I know this is my job, I know I volunteered for this. What a dumb ass.

The formation begins its journey over the channel. Let me get situated. Unlock turret, check. Oxygen, check. Ammunition, check. Intercom, check. The guns are worked up and down. The turret is turned left and right. Guns are charged. POW, POW, POW, POW, POW. The mighty .50s bark out an angry staccato, I am ready.

CRUMPH, CRUMPH, FLAK greets us as we enter Europe. Oh Lord, I dread every mission. Every time we fly, there it is, FLAK. How many times can I take my chances? I will take it like a man. Just let it be quick. Air combat remains the same. What combat? Sitting here waiting to get killed is not combat. I am just a fool in a turret. A fool that thought flying would be romantic. What an idiot!

Brackets of anti-aircraft target the formation. Come on Penny, carry us through this again. We turn on the I.P. to begin the bomb run. Leslie reports, "Bomb bay doors opened." The formation flies straight and level for the sake of hitting the target. The minutes drag on every time. We are sitting ducks. Leslie calls out, "Bombs away." Nick asks, "Bombs away?" Leslie replies, "Check that." Leslie reports, "Yes, we dropped early."

The lead plane dropped early and most of the group followed. We continue the run. The formation reaches the correct release point and the remaining B-24s drop their bombs.

From my perch, I check the results. There are good strikes on the airfield, but not a lot. Off in the distance, a huge column of smoke rises from where the bulk of the formation dropped its bombs. I don't know what we hit, but we bombed the crap out of it.

CRUMPH, CRUMPH, this god damn FLAK will not quit. Come on Penny get us home. Nick reports the lead bomber has been hit. There it is, the wounded aircraft comes into view as it falls back.

Fire streams out of a hole in the wing of this Liberator. What are those guys waiting for? They need to get out now. The wing suddenly snaps off of the B-24. It stands vertical in the air as the plane leans over on its side. The tumbling wing sheers off half of the tail.

Nobody is getting out now. The Liberator starts to careen wildly. It flips and tumbles earthward in violent gyrations. The bomber starts to break up. With a flash, it explodes. All that remains is the familiar crazy, black smoke trail that marks the death of ten men. What once was a bomber rains from the sky.

Oh God, protect us. The anti-aircraft gunners continue to throw brackets at the formation. Come on Penny. Get us out of here. CRUMPH, CRUMPH, Nick jukes across the sky. Mercifully, we emerge from the dark cloud of death. Wow, that was rough. We fly home in an empty sky.

Nick simply follows landmarks across England anymore. We fly a holding pattern until it is our turn to come in. It feels like I've done this a thousand times. There isn't much to be said on the flight deck as we take landing positions.

Luther sets the flaps before we turn on final approach. The kids wave wildly as we touch down. The bomb bay doors are opened as we taxi to our hardstand. The propellers slow to a stop as Penny is shut down.

Major Stewart pulls up in his jeep. He ducks into the bomb bay before any of us can get out. He looks up with a big smile and yells out, "THAT'S IT BOYS, YOU'RE DONE!" *(His voice is just like in the movies.)* Joe Craft turns to me smiling and we shake hands. I turn around to see Nick and Luther laugh as they shake hands.

Major Stewart pats each of us on the back as we emerge from under Penny. With a pat on the shoulder, Major Stewart tells me, "Good job, Fury." I take a good look at our Liberator; she carried us through all of it. I pat her metal body affectionately.

Crew 41 falls to its knees, not so jokingly, kissing the ground. Thanks are given to God for letting us survive our tour. Silent promises are made to the Almighty in payment for letting us live.

The ground crew is ecstatic. They congratulate us with handshakes and pats on the back. The exchanges are mutual. Our ground crew has always had Penny ready to go. There was never a failure on their part. Victory is theirs as well. The thirty-second and final bomb that represents a mission will be painted on Penny later. Thirty-two missions and seven kills, not bad.

Maj. Stewart is truly relieved to see that we have made it. He smiles with satisfaction as he watches his boys gather their flight gear. We are the first crew in the 734th Squadron to finish. Major Stewart tells us, "Come on boys, I'll give you a ride back."

Nick Radosevich and Leslie Lee hop on the hood of the jeep and rest their feet on the bumper. Joe Craft takes a seat on the fender. Carl Powell puts his charts on the passenger seat. Robert Victor hops on back. Laddy Head approaches the jeep with his gear. Luther Clark, Jim Turwilliger, Rob Hansen and I talk as we throw our gear in the back. I look up to see the base photographer snap a picture of us. Our motley crew overloads the jeep as Major Stewart takes us down the flight line.

As we pass the surrounding hardstands, crews undress next to their planes. Some are sullen. Some carry on loudly. Pilots and ground crew inspect damaged bombers. Some planes sit quietly on their pads. They did not fly today. We will never have to do this again. What a nice day, what a wonderful day it is.

At debriefing, we are informed that Major Kemp was in the lead bomber. The events that led to his demise are relayed to the interrogator. All the crew is presumed lost, too bad.

We will receive the Distinguished Flying Cross for successful completion of our missions. All I know is we made it. We took our chances with Penny and survived. "Lucky Penny" was just that.

With a newfound freedom, we walk to the mess hall. Charlie makes us something in celebration. The food tastes great. We go to our shack and clean up. Tonight, we celebrate.

In the heart of the night, we sit in the pub with drinks in hand. We toast to our survival. We drink to beating the odds. We toast our pilot. We toast the locals in the pub. We thank God. The guys rib me about praying all the time, but here we are. Yes, we made it. Crew 41 of the original cadre has survived. No more will we fly in the 734th squadron of the 453rd Bomb Group. We revel through the night.

8. THAT'S IT BOY'S, YOU'RE DONE!

The sun of a new day shines in the barracks window. I have survived. Crew 41 has made it. No more crossing the English Channel. My tour of Germany, France, Holland, Belgium and Denmark is over. Last night, that is a different story. It was rough, but we made it.

There is a new outlook on life. We are issued leaves. We will attack London tonight. The guards at the gate congratulate us on finishing our tour. Laddy, Joe and I hop a train bound for London in Attleboro. We swear to not do anything stupid, or get ourselves killed.

As soon as the train stops, we go straight to Piccadilly Circus. Drinks are raised in the nearest pub. I tell the guys I gotta go. They know what I am up to. My girlfriend's flat is the objective. A smiling face answers a knock on the door. She undresses as I drag her across the floor. We flop onto the bed and start rolling around.

The sound of a wailing air raid siren breaks the mood. Holy crap, a V-1 Buzz Bomb. Its distinct sound cannot be mistaken. The pulsating drone of its engine grows louder. I stumble to the door trying to dress at the same time.

My girl lays naked on the bed laughing at me. "Come on, lets go," I blurt out. She replies, "If you get it, you get it." My reply to her is, "Not me, god dammit. I just made it. I am not going to die now." I can understand the mentality. London has been bombed since 1939, but my God!

Anti-aircraft fire targets the V-1 in an attempt to bring it down. The Buzz Bomb's engine going silent quickens my pace to the bomb shelter. A huge explosion that makes the ground tremble goes off in the distance.

The V-1 has found its target. A small part of London is reduced to rubble. Moments later, the air raid siren wails out the all clear. I hurry back to my girl's flat. She lays on the bed waiting. She giggles as I shake my head laughing. I leave a trail of clothes behind me.

After a few days, Crew 41 returns to Old Buck. The eleventh crewmember does not haunt us. It feels great to not be shadowed by that specter anymore.

I am now assigned to the flight line. I like doing this stuff. I am around the planes, but I do not have to fly. It is easy work. It reminds me of Seymour Johnson. My job is to drive the bulldozer that sits at the end of the runway until my orders for home come through. I wonder where I will be stationed.

We are moved out of our barracks so a replacement crew can take their chances. I wonder how much longer it will take the Carter crew to finish.

We still eat in the aircrew mess hall and I ignore every new face I see. I don't want to know anybody. I wonder who will make it. There is absolutely no way to tell. Fate will take care of that. The new crews stare at our jackets. We wear them like badges of honor. They tell a story of survival, missions flown. We are proof you can make it.

After a few weeks of working the line, my papers finally come through. I will be sailing home on the R.M.S. Queen Mary. I have a 24 day leave to do what I want when I return to the States. I will then proceed to Westover, MA and fly A-26 Invaders. That's good, I will be near home. It will be nice to see my mom and sisters. I will get to see Helen, too.

I wonder how my brother is doing. I pray I will see him again. I hope nothing crazy happens. I pray the Krauts don't drag him out and shoot him. I hope we don't bomb him. He is such a dumb ass. I am going to kill him after this is over. Oh well, at least we have troops on the ground. Maybe we will win the war. At least one of mom's boys is coming home.

The now Col. Hubbard calls us to order. He was our original pilot. After a short ceremony, we are decorated with the Distinguished Flying Cross for successful completion of each of our missions. We are given this award for our courage and exceptional skill displayed in the face of the enemy. After we are dismissed, Laddy, Joe and I go pick up our laundry for the last time.

We take the dog for a slow walk to the house of our favorite lady. With a knock on the door, she lets us in. We take our clothes and give her some rations. We tell her we have finished our tour and will be going home. Delighted at the news of our good fortune, she gives each of us a teary-eyed hug.

I tell the boy I have a surprise for him. I bend over and hand him our dog's leash. I tell Penny to go to him. I tell the boy, "He is a good dog. He even flew a mission with us. Take good care of him." We each pet our little black Cocker Spaniel one last time.

Penny watches us leave. He is now a resident of England. He will be happy with the boy. We spend the rest of the day at the base preparing for home. Tomorrow we begin to go our separate ways. Personal belongings are gathered up before we hit the sack. Thoughts of Helen fill my mind as I drift off.

I am awakened by the sound of a lone voice. Activity can be heard in the distance. Muffled voices can be heard as men prepare for a mission. Doors and gates slam, truck engines rev.

I stare into the darkness and listen. In the distance, the familiar sound of an engine coughing to life is no more than a whisper. Moments later, it is joined by the faint sound of another engine turning over. Another engine coughs to life nearby. The drone of an awakening airbase splits the quite of the night.

Engines are run up to full throttle then set at idle. The sound of B-24s taxiing out of their hardstands, and down the ramp, fill the predawn air. Bombers idle as they wait at the end of the ramps for the signal to go.

I listen to the sound of planes taking flight. I listen to every last one. The sound of the formation circling overhead penetrates the shadowy darkness of dawn. I lay in my bunk listening to the formation fade into the distance. Sleep steals me back as Old Buck waits for her bombers to return.

Under the morning sun, the crew musters in front of the barracks. Nick gathers us around one last time. He tells us we are a good crew. He is proud of us and would fly anywhere with us. We put our trust in Nick and he piloted us through all our missions. I tell Luther, "You are a damn good pilot." He is a hell of a pilot. Nick and Luther saved our lives over Siracourt. Nick not so jokingly tells me, "Your prayers saved our lives more than you know."

We exchange home addresses. I don't know if any of us will actually get in touch with each other, but we have the means to do so.

Crew 41 will be completely dismantled in a few days. We will be no more than a memory. It does hurt to leave the guys. I do love my crew. It is a love that was borne of facing death together. We never speak of it, but we will be bound to each other until the day we die.

After spending one last day at Old Buck, it is time to go. My newly shined shoes look good with my Class A uniform. I make sure my diary, map, good luck doll and pieces of shrapnel are in my duffle bag. I can't believe the wrinkles on my face, and my toes occasionally hurt. I wonder if they will be a problem the rest of my life.

Sitting on the edge of my bunk, I know things are different now. It feels like I have lived a lifetime in six months. Nobody will understand what I went through unless they have been here themselves. Who are they to say? Why should I say anything about it and be judged by somebody that was not here?

I have seen men die. I have lived in constant fear. I am a witness to things that are hard to explain. I have been shot at and I have killed. I got that dirty bastard over Gotha and I hit that one passing through the formation. I know I got him, he dove away smoking. I have dropped bombs on people, and I have no regrets. I am a survivor.

I share a last cigarette with the guys as I wait for my ride into Attleboro. Arrangements have been made to hitch a ride with two orderlies into town. I throw my duffle bag in the back of the jeep and hop in.

At the gate, the guard tells me, "I see you are finally dressed properly." We laugh and I tell him, "I am going home." He tells me, "Good Luck!" I am saluted by the M.P. as I drive away. A final look is given to Old Buck as I travel down the road for the last time.

I am told, "Good luck," as I am dropped off at the train

station. Local passengers and a few airmen mill about the platform. They are heading to London on leave. "How many missions do you have to go?" I am asked. I reply, "I am finished, I am going home." Their faces cannot hide what they are thinking; will they make it home too? We ride together to London. I tell the guys, "Good luck," as we get off the train.

The first thing I have to do is go to my girls flat. I'd like to tell her goodbye. Nobody answers the door, and I have to go. I know it is not right, but maybe it's better this way. I know I will never see her again.

For the first time, I am a tourist in London. For all the times I have been to Piccadilly Circus, I have never really looked around. I have some time, I'll browse the shops. I wander into a coat store. There are some nice kid's coats my sisters would like. They are good quality. I have them boxed for the journey home.

After roaming the shops of London for a while, I have to move on. I catch a train for the two hour ride to the docks of South Hampton. That is where the Queen Mary waits.

The Queen Mary is a big ship. She has three huge smoke stacks sticking out of her. I show my orders and proceed up the gangplank. Wow, from where I stand it must be over three stories high to the deck.

Once aboard, I am instructed to find a bunk. This will be my home until we reach America. After stowing my gear away, a stroll of the deck is in order. There are guys from all branches of the service milling about. Everybody is cordial, happy to be going home.

I watch a group of black uniformed German prisoners as they are marched into the ships hold. They appear to be SS. One of the prisoners turns to a guard and mumbles something. The reply is a butt stroke to the small of his back. The force of the blow drives the prisoner to his knees. The British soldier urges him on with the threat of another. The Nazi struggles to his feet and stumbles forward. Everybody that witnesses the episode curses the Krauts, or tells the British guards to give it to the bastards.

These German prisoners will be taken to the United States. We have prisoner of war camps in Arizona, Mississippi and Arkansas, to name a few. These camps are in the middle of nowhere. An escapee has nowhere to go. In a place like Arizona, there is nothing but the desert.

German submarine crews that were captured in the North Atlantic were the first to be interned in the United States. The camps started filling up when Rommel's Africa Corps was defeated. Now the prisoners are the troops we captured in Italy and the invasion of France. For the most part, the die-hard Nazi's are sent to America.

Destroyers escort our convoy. They screen us as we zig-zag across the Atlantic. I search the skies at the sound of an aircraft. It is a sub chasing PBY patrolling above us. Every precaution is taken to protect the convoy from a submarine attack. To be sunk by a Kraut now would really suck. What a way to go, survive 32 missions and wind up being torpedoed on the way home.

The days are past watching guys play cards or shoot craps. Wads of money exchange hands on a regular basis. There is always somebody around to strike up a conversation with. Hours are spent sharing stories of combat or talking about future plans.

The night brings the occasional scream from a soldier reliving his personal combat horror. Hearing this makes me think too. I tell myself, "It is over." I tell myself, "You made it." The days and nights pass as the convoy slowly works its way home.

The ships of the convoy have stopped their constant zig-zagging. I am told we are nearing New York City. About an hour later someone on the deck yells out, "Land ho, there it is!" The Statue of Liberty and the New York skyline come into view.

The sound of celebration breaks out, it fills the air. We pass Lady Liberty as the Queen Mary goes to dock. I have made it home. I gaze at the Statue of Liberty as she looks back at Europe.

The 453rd fills my thoughts. I think about the guys. Boy, oh boy. What a crew. I wonder who is flying "Lucky

Penny II" now. I wonder if she has been shot down.

I do take pride in knowing that I fought for freedom. I have carried the war to those that would take freedom away. I hope the sacrifice I have witnessed will secure a future of peace. I pray I don't have to go to the Pacific. I know the war isn't over but we are winning on both fronts. It appears if I go anywhere, it will be in an A-26 Invader.

I have been tested and survived. I am a warrior. The things I have done will always be with me. I may have to do it again. I pray I do not.

I have discovered the hellish creature war is. Even though it is simplistic, a part of me is proud to have fought for what the Statue of Liberty stands for. "Lucky Penny" carried her message half a world away.

EPILOGUE

Edmund *(Black Fury)* Survilla went home to his mom and sisters. He surprised them on an early afternoon. He then went to Helen's house and spent the day with her. The next 24 days were spent with his family and gal.

Edmund then reported to Westover, MA for A-26 Invader training. He was assigned as a gunner on the attack variant of this aircraft. His duty was to operate the 75mm cannon that is mounted in the nose of the Invader. He sat on what equates to a bicycle seat, next to the pilot. From there he would operate the cannon.

He met and dated an Admiral's daughter until it became too contentious. The mother was a drunk and the father was away at war. She was a cute little blonde, but there was too much baggage.

Edmund did not go overseas again. He flew practice missions up and down the Mid Atlantic coast until he was discharged.

He returned to Luzerne, PA, and worked as an assistant in an auto upholstery shop. He married Helen and had three daughters.

Edmund opened an auto upholstery shop of his own in Hazleton, PA. After running the shop in Hazleton for three years, he moved his family to Drums, PA. He eventually moved his auto upholstery business to Drums also. He ran his shop for 46 years.

Edmund was involved in the VFW, girl's softball and the local fire company. His passions were golf and hunting. After Edmund finished his military flying, he never stepped foot in an airplane again.

My friend, Edmund M. Survilla, died October 2, 2008. The light grows dimmer.

Staff Sergeant Survilla's tribute to the fighter escorts.
(Taken from his diary).

This page is set aside to honor our fighter escort.

It is great to see those guys up there watching over the formation. You're like a kid when you go to a cowboy show, and when the bandits are rounded up by the sheriff, you cheer. It's the same way up there over enemy territory. You cheer and say a prayer at the same time. Once in a while, you see them break up their formation, and a short while later, you see a Jerry go down in flames or if he is lucky, he bails out. All we ask for is a fighter escort, and the Lord's watchful eye. They're like your guardian angel watching over you.

NOTES

THE GOOD LUCK DOLL - Edmund returned his good luck doll to the W.A.C.s after he came home. He had every mission that he had flown marked on it. His doll was discovered in the 1990's and he was made aware of its existence.

THE SHRAPNEL - The shrapnel that Edmund picked out of "Lucky Penny's" tail sat in a cookie jar in the kitchen of his home until the day he died.

THE MAP - The map that Edmund drew Penny's missions on was taken *(stolen)* by a teacher when one of his daughters brought it to school for show and tell.

EDMUND'S FLIGHT GEAR - His brother gave the leather jacket *(with "Lucky Penny" and missions on it)*, goggles and helmet away.

EDMUND'S BROTHER - Edmund's brother was a radio operator on a B-24. He survived the war as a P.O.W. He was liberated by Patton's troops in the closing weeks.

This is his account:

We were shot up by a Me-262. The pilot told us to bail out. I turned to the top turret gunner and said, "Let's go!" I jumped out the bomb bay, and that's the last time I saw him. I watched my plane start to go down and explode.

EDMUND'S CONFIRMED KILL - Luftwaffe wartime records confirm, JG-26 *(The Abbeville Kids)* lost four fighters on February 24, 1944.

Edmund's gun camera reel would read, 2-24-1944. Ssgt. Edmund M. Survilla, Serial # 3358551, 453rd Bomb Group, 734th Squadron, "Lucky Penny" tail gun.

CREW 41 of LUCKY PENNY

Pilot -	Lieutenant - Nicholas Radosevich
Co Pilot -	Lieutenant - Luther M. Clark
Navigator *	Lieutenant - Joseph Miller
Navigator -	Lieutenant - Carl Powell
Bombardier *	Lieutenant - Robert E. Burgess
Bombardier -	Lieutenant - Leslie Lee
Top Turret -	Sergeant - Robert O. Hansen
Ball Turret -	Sergeant - Laddy P. Head
Waist Gunner -	Sergeant- Robert E. Victor
Waist Gunner -	Sergeant - James Turwilliger
Radio Operator -	Sergeant - Joseph D. Craft
Tail Gunner -	Sergeant - Edmund M. Survilla

(* transferred to another crew after arriving in England.)

LUCKY PENNY

"LUCKY PENNY", B-24H, Serial # 42-52169 went into action, 2-4-1944. Flew 23 missions, 16 with her crew. Shot down, 5-8-1944 over Brunswick, Germany."Lucky Penny" was painted olive drab upper, grey lower. White roundels were painted on the tail and wing surfaces. Black Js were painted in the roundels. J+ radio call letters were painted white under the roundels on the tail. E8 was painted aft of the waist gunner position in white. A black Cocker Spaniel riding a falling bomb was painted on the pilot's side of the nose. "Lucky Penny" was written above the dog riding the bomb in white. Crew member names were painted under the top turret. Missions and kills were painted under the cockpit on the pilot's side.

(Note - There is a picture of "Lucky Penny" in the book, In Search of Peace, by Micheal D. Bednarcik. A different crew stands in front of her, but the dog is visible riding the bomb.)

LUCKY PENNY II

"LUCKY PENNY II", B-24J, Serial # 42-95312, went into action, 5-13-1944. Flew 63 missions, 14 with her crew. Shot down, 10-17-1944 over Cologne, Germany. It was natural metal with black vertical tail surfaces. A white stripe was painted diagonally through the tail surfaces. The call letter J+ was painted black inside the white stripe. The white roundel with black J remained on the wing. E8 was painted in black aft of the waist gunner windows. "Lucky Penny II" was painted on both sides of the nose in black. Crew names were painted under the top turret. Missions and kills were painted under the cockpit on the pilot's side.

(Note - There is also a picture of "Lucky Penny II" in the book, In Search of Peace, by Michael D. Bednarcik.)

The Missions of Crew #41

# 1	February 13th.	Siracourt, France.
# 2	February 24th.	Gotha, Germany
# 3	February 25th.	Furth, Germany
# 4	March 5th.	Cazaux, France
# 5	March 6th.	Berlin, Germany
# 6	March 8th.	Berlin, Germany
# 7	March 15th.	Brunswick, Germany
# 8	March 16th.	Friedrichshafen, Germany
# 9	March 18th.	Friedrichshafen, Germany
#10	March 23rd.	Munster, Germany
#11	March 26th.	Domart, France
#12	March 27th.	Pau, France
#13	April 8th.	Brunswick, Germany
#14	April 9th.	Tutow, Germany
#15	April 10th.	Tours, France
#16	April 18th.	Tutow, Germany
#17	April 30th.	Siracourt, France
#18	May 1st.	Watten, France
*	May 2nd.	Siracourt, France
#19	May 13th.	Tutow, *(Poland)* Germany
#20	May 15th.	Siracourt, France
#21	May 19th.	Brunswick, Germany
#22	May 20th.	Reims, France
#23	May 22nd.	Orleans, France
#24	May 25th.	Troyes, France
#25	May 28th.	Merseburg, Germany
#26	May 31st.	Lumes, France
#27	June 4th.	Romorantin, France
#28	June 5th.	Invasion Points
#29	June 6th.	Invasion Points
#30	June 8th.	Flers, France
#31	June 10th.	Boulogne, France
#32	June 11th.	Cormeilles, France

(* makeup mission)

A FEW QUESTIONS

I asked Edmund - Did you think you would make it?

Edmund - No, I lived for today for the most part. I did my womanizing and living it up.

I asked Edmund - Were you scared?

Edmund - Yes, there were a few moments I was terrified. Anybody that says they were not is lying or crazy. Some of it still seems like yesterday. I still have dreams about it.

I asked Edmund - What is the worst part of aerial combat?

Edmund - FLAK, there isn't anywhere to hide in the sky. You cannot shoot back at it. You just sit there and take it.

I asked Edmund - Did you know you were making history on D-Day?

Edmund - No, we were just doing our job.

I asked Edmund - How do you feel about the German you shot down on the Gotha mission?

Edmund - I got you, you bastard. We had survived that flat spin the mission before *(Siracourt),* and I knew it was for keeps after that.

I asked Edmund - Did the Carter crew make it?

Edmund - Yes.

I asked Nick Radosevich - Did you think you were going to make it?

Nick - I always knew we would make it.

*(**Note** - Airmen of World War II were just as foul mouthed as any other twenty year old. The profanity has been kept at a bare minimum for the sake of this book.)*

DEFINITIONS

Aileron, A control surface on the trailing edge of a wing used to turn or control the attitude of an aircraft.

Bomb Group, A bomber unit of the Air Force that contains multiple squadrons.

Brown Out, A term used to describe when fear causes a person to lose control of their bowels.

Bunching, A maneuver bomb groups used to assemble for a mission. The bombers fly in a large circular pattern until all planes take their assigned position in a formation.

Buzz Bomb, A self-propelled, guided missile (*resembling an aircraft*) used by Germany to attack England.

Cadre, A core of men and officers necessary to establish a new unit. The members of the cadre started the new bomb group.

CHAFF, Thin metalized strips of material that reflect radar signals *(creating false echoes).* It was used as a countermeasure against enemy radar.

Combat Box, A defensive formation built of **Elements** that are arranged for maximum protection.

Contrails, (*slang*) Condensation Trails. A visible trail caused by the hot air of an engines exhaust colliding with the cold air of the atmosphere. When conditions are right, the hot air condenses and freezes forming ice crystals. The result is long, thin clouds that emanate from an aircraft's exhaust.

Cowl Flaps, Hinged surfaces on the trailing edge of an engine cowling. (*The flaps open and close to regulate engine temperature.*)

Crabbing, A maneuver used to compensate for the drift of an aircraft caused by a crosswind.

Element, A three plane formation that flies in a V pattern.

Engine Nacelle, A streamlined enclosure around an aircraft engine.

Escort, To accompany, to protect. The fighters escorted the bombers.

FLAK, A term commonly used by WWII Allied Airmen to describe German anti-aircraft artillery. It is an acronym for the German words, **FL**iger **A**bwehr **K**anone. *(Flier, Defence, Cannon)* This loosely translates to, air defense cannon.

Flight Deck, A place where the pilot and co-pilot are stationed in an aircraft. An aircraft is piloted from here.

Gyro, A device that is used to define a fixed direction in space or to determine the attitude of an aircraft.

Hardstand, A prepared surface for an aircraft to park on.

Invasion Stripes, 18 inch wide white and black alternating stripes that were painted vertically on the fuselage and wing surfaces of Allied aircraft. These stripes were applied to all fighter and medium bombers for easy identification during the invasion of France. *(Operation Overlord, D-Day.)*

I.P., *(abbr.)* **I**nitial **P**oint, a designated spot chosen on a map for the bombers to begin their attack. It is no more than a selected location in the sky.

Kentucky Windage, The practice of shooting at a target instinctively. A person estimates the speed and direction of a target without the use of any mechanical aids.

Ma Duce, *(slang),* The affectionate name given to the Browning .50 caliber machine gun.

Marker Bomb, A bomb that trails smoke when released. It was used to signal the accompanying planes when to drop their bombs.

Marshalling Yard, A place where rail cars are stored and lined up to make trains. Locomotives are also repaired and stored here when not in use.

Pitot Tube, A tube facing into the airstream attached to an instrument that measures air pressure.

Astro-Dome, A transparent dome on top of an aircraft through which celestial readings can be taken to navigate an aircraft. On a B-24, it is located on top of the aircraft between the nose and flight deck.

Strafing, To attack by aircraft with machine guns. Usually, low level attacks on targets such as troops, convoys, trains, airfields, etc. The word strafe is derived from the German word Strafen *(to punish).* Allied pilots of WWII made this word common.

Smoke Pot, A generic term used to describe any smoke generating device. A machine that creates a cloud *(smoke screen)* to conceal a target.

Turret Well, A place where the Ball Turret is stowed when retracted in a B-24 Liberator.

W.A.C., Women's Army Corps. The female branch of the Army Air Corps during World War II.

Zuyder Zee, A shallow bay of the North Sea located off of the northwest coast of the Netherlands.

REFERENCES

This book would not exist if it were not for Edmund M. Survilla. I would not trade the two and a half years of listening to him recount his military service for anything. I am honored that he chose me to tell it all. His photos brought words to life.

Edmund Survilla's diary, He had the foresight to list and date each mission that he flew.

Nicholas Radosevich, I would like to thank him for the brief conversations we had pertaining to his plane and crew.

Andrew Strasko, S1/c, U.S. Navy, 1942-1945. U.S.S. Quincy, CA-39, CA-71. 7th Division. Shelled Gold Beach on D-Day. I would like to thank him for describing how a naval bombardment is carried out.

Michael D. Bednarcik, In Search of Peace. A complete history of the 453rd Bomb Group.

Pilot Training Manual for the B-24 Liberator. U.S.A.A.C. Copifier Lithograph Corp. Cleveland, OH. October 1944. 28,000.

Pilot Training Manual for the A-26 Invader. U.S.A.A.C. Copifier Lithograph Corp. Cleveland, OH. January 1945. 7000.

Roger A. Freeman, The Mighty Eighth, *(Costa Mesa, CA: Jane's, 1981.)*

Paul E. Eden & Soph Moeng, Aircraft Anatomy of World War II, *(London, U.K.: Aerospace Publishing, Ltd, 2003.)*

Werner Baumbach, The Life and Death of the Luftwaffe, *(New York, NY: Ballentine Books, 1967.)*

Cajus Dekker, The Luftwaffe Diaries, *(New York, NY: Ballentine Books, 1969.)*

Jeffery L. Ethell, Air Command - Fighters and Bombers of World War II, *(Ann Arbor, MI: Borders, Inc., 1997.)*

Martin Caidin, Flying Forts, *(New York, NY: Ballentine Books, 1968.)* Thunderbolt!, 7th Edition, *(New York, NY: Ballentine Books, 1979.)* Fork-Tailed Devil, *(New York, NY: Ballentine Books, 1971.)*

William Hess, P-51 Bomber Escort - A century of warfare, *(New York, NY: Ballentine Books, 1971.)*

Ken Nellis, (*web site*) 453rd BG (H). http:// tin pan. fortune city.com/april skies/ 264.old buck. html.

ACKNOWLEDGEMENTS

No man is an island. I owe a debt of gratitude to Attorney James R. Scallion. His assistance and input have been instrumental.

I would like to thank Katie Barton *(paralegal),* for her patience and assistance with this project.

I would like to thank David Leitner for his contribution towards the completion of this book.

I would like to thank Albert Antolick for his contribution in support of this book.

I would like to thank my wife Eileen and my daughter Athena for all their support in this endeavor.   *F.S.H.S.*